SERIOUS

SERIOUSLY RICH

HOW THE DISCOVERY OF TREASURE TURNED A LIFE OF WASTE INTO WEALTH

Richard Pidgley

AUTHENTIC BOOKS
Milton Keynes, England

First published 2002 by Authentic Books, a division of
Authentic Media, 9 Holdom Avenue, Bletchley, Milton
Keynes, Bucks, MK1 1QR, UK
Distributed in the USA by Gabriel Resources,
PO Box 1047, Waynesboro GA 30830-2047

British Library Cataloguing in Publication Data

A catalogue record for this book is available from the British
Library

1-86024-280-4

Cover design by David Lund
Printed in Great Britain by
Cox and Wyman Ltd., Reading, Berkshire

DEDICATION

I would like to dedicate this book to my wife Lynne, who is my best friend and has made many sacrifices in order to help me fulfil my call in God.

Who can find a virtuous and capable wife? She is worth more than precious rubies. Her husband can trust her, and she will greatly enrich his life. She will not hinder him but help him all her life. . . . She is energetic and strong, a hard worker. She watches for bargains; her lights burn late into the night. . . . Her children stand and bless her. Her husband praises her: 'There are many virtuous and capable women in the world, but you surpass them all!'

Proverbs 31

CONTENTS

ACKNOWLEDGEMENTS

I would like to thank my friends Pat Collyer, Jerry and Jackie Geatches and Reverend Ramon Hunston for their help and encouragement in writing this book. Also, special thanks to Pastor Albert and Peggy Garner – mentors and friends. And finally, a big thankyou to all my friends at Robinswood Pentecostal Church who believed in this book and who have supported me from its conception to completion.

This book is a true account of my life. However, some names have been changed and place names omitted to protect the privacy of those who I have mentioned in the book.

FOREWORD

'You are familiar with the generosity of our Master, Jesus Christ. Rich as he was, he gave it all away for us – in one stroke he became poor and we became rich.' [1]

The grace of God is stunning. God's grace links us with his plans that began before time was created and extend beyond the end of time. God's grace lifts us from the depths of human despair to the delights of a relationship with the Father. God's grace liberates us from slavery to the deception and ugliness of sin into the freedom and beauty of his love. And God's grace makes us rich – seriously rich!

God's grace is not found in theological textbooks but in human hearts. God's grace is not a philosophical conclusion made by some irrelevant ecclesiastical council: it is the power of God that transforms hearts and lives. God's grace turns sinners into saints, rebels into royalty and miscreants into ministers. Sin always brings poverty to the human heart, but grace brings God's riches that makes a person rich – seriously rich!

God's grace is personal, lavished upon the world, yet equally applied to individual lives. The story of Richard Pidgley demonstrates the power of God's grace that can reach the individual. What the grace of God has done in Richard's life demonstrates to us all that no need is too great, no place too far, no pit too deep and no moment too late for the grace of God.

Richard Pidgley is a fellow minister of the Gospel. He is a good friend and a brother. And he is seriously rich!

Jeremy Griffiths
Founder and President
The Shepherd's Storehouse International

INTRODUCTION

I was born on the 5 February 1966 in Poole, Dorset. I didn't come into the world on my own, because not long after I was born, Colin my twin brother also arrived. My family was plagued by many problems such as crime, gambling and drink. As a toddler I was not aware of the full extent of my parents' petty criminal empire, but as I grew older more was revealed to me. According to my mum, my real dad disputed his fatherhood of Colin and me. He blamed our arrival on somebody such as the milkman! So, with this major difficulty in the marriage, my parents decided to break up: I was 18 months old. This resulted in Colin and me being placed in various foster homes, sometimes together and sometimes apart.

This book is a true account of my life, one that started in a broken home and led to a dank prison cell. I have been honest in recalling my life as it happened. I have no wish to glorify my past, but have written in such a way that you, the reader, can comprehend the wonderful change that has taken place since Jesus Christ came into my heart. This book relates how I discovered true treasure in Jesus Christ: a treasure that turned my ruined life of shame and waste into wealth, literally overnight!

This is a story that will inspire genuine hope for all
those from broken homes, hope for those held prisoners
to sin, hope for those desperately looking for love and
acceptance, hope for parents worried about their children
who are on drugs and into crime. As the words of the
song writer said . . .

> It is no secret what God can do
> What he's done for others, he can do for you.[2]

The Bible declares: *'Those who become Christians become
new persons. They are not the same anymore, for the old life is
gone. A new life has begun!'*[3]

1

EARLY DAYS

Terry and Sally Smith were a couple in their forties, who had never been able to have children of their own. Because of their love for children they became foster parents, and in this they excelled. Thinking back over the years, I can remember them telling us of many other children who they had counted it a privilege to foster. They had had children from deprived areas of London for summer holidays by the seaside and also longer-term placements.

Terry was a carpenter, and a very good one at that. He had a large garage by the side of the house filled with tools and was always doing little jobs for people. He worked for a company by Poole Quay and was the yard foreman. My fond memories of him were of a man who was gentle and peace loving. I never heard him quarrel with people, but felt his hurt as he became upset when others fought and fell out. He was a great lover of going along steadily, 'keeping his nose clean' as he put it. He was strict when he needed to be and I can remember going over his knees on more than one occasion for a spanking, which I am sure I rightly deserved! Terry didn't have any hobbies as such, for most of his spare time was spent looking after his aged mum and two aunts. He would chop firewood for them and mow their lawns. Almost every Saturday night we would all go with him to visit the family. After doing all the chores, with which I would help him, Terry would sit down in a well-worn armchair and listen to the family news from the lips of his mum or aunts. They loved to look after him as well, making him supper of ham sandwiches and home-made bread pudding that he enjoyed so much.

Sally was a mum to me – I went to her screaming with my first bee sting! I went to her with sticky fingers to wipe, and she would sit by my bed many a night waiting for me to drop off to sleep. She just loved children: black, white or yellow it didn't matter. She would spend hours with all sorts of kids. We must have worn her out – she wasn't getting any younger – as we wanted to do this and that. But she took it all in her stride, and I know now that we aged both her and Terry. She never moaned about her rights as an individual in the home, making sacrifices all the time so the rest of us had what we needed. I am glad though now – years on from the nightmare of my youth – that I can still pick up the phone and call her 'Mum'.

Both Terry and Sally Smith gave us love and welcomed us into their home. They did what they could to help two little boys find the love and acceptance that all children need. As we grew, so did the pressures on that little home, pressure that Terry and Sally's health finally couldn't cope with. I want to honour them, along with all foster parents who give their lives selflessly to children, doing all that they possibly can. Often they are hurt and abused by the system. Often they are financially worse off. Tired

> *I want to honour them along with all foster parents who give their lives selflessly to children*

physically and mentally, but loving children all the same, they do it all just to see the smiles upon their little faces.

Colin and I were very young when we were placed with the Smiths: so young I can't remember accurately much before that time. One of my earliest memories at the Smiths' was being pushed in a pushchair beside a duck pond. I was allowed out of the buggy and toddled by the waterside held securely by a rein, which was leather with a little blue breastplate. The sun was shining, the memories of whatever had happened before were clouded, and for now I was happy, secure in the love that Terry and Sally Smith were giving me.

I can remember being bathed in the kitchen sink! I guess I was pretty small then, as I sat in that sink playing with a cup and splashing around in what seemed to be gallons of water. I remember that, along with millions of other kids, I hated the soap getting in my eyes. Mrs Smith would be as careful as she could, but paranoia would set in and screams would be heard! I laugh now as I bathe Sam, my youngest son, and hear him squeal as he too hates the soap getting near his face.

I can remember being bathed in the kitchen sink

The Smiths loved us and for a while everything looked as if it would work out wonderfully. We had settled in well and so, after a few years, the Smiths wanted to make the arrangement more secure and permanent for them and also for Colin and me. They applied to adopt us, and so the wheels began to move as social workers and other professionals made their assessments. The whole thing would have been a 'happy ever after' story except for one thing. That one thing proved

> *The whole thing would have been a 'happy ever after' story except for one thing*

to be an obstacle that nobody was going to be able to remove. My real mother!

She had been allowed access to Colin and me every now and again. In fact, I didn't think of her as my mum at all. We would be taken to a social services office in lower parkstone. Once, after trust had been built, the social worker would allow her to walk Colin and me in the small park. I can remember all her questions about Terry and Sally Smith and whether we were happy there or not. She would bring different presents for us on those trips in a bid to buy affection, but no matter how many gifts she brought, which I later found out were stolen, I could not bring myself to like her. I would feel uncomfortable and would recoil from her as she went to kiss and hug me at the end of the visits. Years later when I questioned her about this time in my life, she told me that although she knew both Colin and I were happy at the Smiths and that it would have been the best for us, she couldn't let go of us. She said she resented the Smiths having us and was jealous of them. When the final decision on adoption was made, the answer was no, because of my mother's unwillingness to let us go – although she would not have been able to have us herself at the time.

That was a blow to Terry and Sally, as they had done such a good job with two little boys. We were part of their family and treated as such by all their relatives. The Smiths wanted the security of adoption, as they didn't want the hurt of having us, who they regarded as their sons, torn from them.

Their desire to have their own child legally led them to approach the social services regarding the possibility of having another child. The day came when two suddenly became three! Natalie, a beautiful girl, just two years old, came into the home one day and Colin and I found ourselves with a sister. Things seemed to work out well, as we took to Natalie and played with her for hours, just as any other young family would do. But unbeknown to me, storm clouds were gathering on the horizon all the time.

Springdale Infant School

The day the playgroup took us to see Springdale Infant School was a challenge to my security. It's not fair; as soon as you get used to something like the familiar sights and sounds of a playgroup, they whisk you off to a very different and even threatening place. I had grown to enjoy playgroup and liked all the teachers. I was confident in the surrounds of the United Reformed Church hall and would often don a large tall hat and cape and go around kissing all the ladies much to everyone's amusement! Nothing stays the same for long though, and before I knew it, a teacher had come from the infant school to read us all a story and also to introduce herself. The next week came round and we found ourselves on a guided tour of the school, being shown all the classrooms and playgrounds that we would be using the very next term.

Once I had settled into school my confidence rose, and before long I had made new friends with children who had come from other broadstone playgroups. In fact, I rapidly became a gang leader, which wasn't bad for a kid of my age. My gang was highly feared by the other children because we had this great game called 'Charge of the light brigade'. I would gather my mounted lancers at one end of the playing field and we would put the fine dusty dirt into the pockets of our shorts. Then, at my command of 'Charge', we would run from one side of the field to the other, leaping over and running through any group of children playing in our way. We would also sprinkle the dirt from our pockets as we charged, to give the authentic dust cloud coming from the horses' hooves. This game I had invented was fun for my gang, but not much fun for anyone in our way! The dinner ladies tried to stop us charging around, but rebellion was setting in and I took no notice of their constant appeals to calm down or threats of having to sit inside during playtimes.

> *My gang was highly feared by the other children*

Thief

On the whole, I wasn't too badly behaved – or so I thought! But the day soon came when I was publicly branded a thief before the whole school. I had gone into the school office one lunchtime to see a teacher and discovered that no one was there. I spotted a first aid box open on the office desk. Looking inside, I saw a tube with a lid on that looked pretty interesting: so interesting in fact that I whipped it out of the box and stuffed it in my shorts' pocket. Out in the school playing field, I found a quiet corner and proceeded to examine my 'booty'. Inside the tube was a glass thing that I later learned was a rather expensive thermometer. Curious about the 'red stuff' inside, I smashed the glass vial only to see the red liquid quickly soak into the hot dry ground of the field. I suddenly heard the school bell signifying the end of lunch break. Shoving the plastic tube down the front of my shorts this time, I ran to the yard and lined up with my class waiting to be led into the building by a teacher.

Suddenly my heart stopped. Could I be hearing correctly? They were calling my name out and telling me to come to the front of the school parade. Standing in front of all the other kids, the deputy head, a male teacher, lifted up my shirt and pulled out the plastic tube that had protected the thermometer and held it high for all to see. I was now shamed, and I knew I had done something very wrong. I was then escorted by the deputy head to the headmistresses office and questioned about my crime. To make matters worse, Mrs Smith was called up to the school and, after I had promised to pay back the cost of a new thermometer out of my pocket money, I was taken home early that day in disgrace.

Although I was settled at the Smiths, I was confused when letters were sent from the school to home. Often in the classroom they would read out the surnames of the parents and the appropriate child would cry out 'yes' and raise their hand up to receive the envelope to take home. When they read out 'Mr and Mrs Smith' I had to respond, but because they were called Smith and my name was Pidgley, I felt very uncomfortable and wondered what everyone else was thinking. I hated those times, squirming in my chair feeling hot and bothered, faced flushed as the teacher began calling out surnames beginning with 'S'. Although things were happy at the Smith's home, deep inside my heart the feelings of anxiety and questions like 'Who am I?' rose to the surface. They threatened my little world and made me insecure and often robbed me of many hours of sleep. I remember to this day Mrs Smith sitting by my bedside for hours trying to get me to go to sleep. She knew I was troubled, but all her loving coaxing could not bring me to vocalise my deepest fears.

2

GROWING PAINS

Bandit

The 'egg farm' was about two miles or so away from where we lived. It was a type of farm shop that was little more than a tottering wooden shack at the end of a dusty lane. The outside didn't promise much, but, on entering the shed, a small child was faced with all the delights of Aladdin's cave! For there were shelves of sweets, mojos, blackjacks, fruit salads, sherbet fountains and then those unattainable chocolate delights that our pocket money could never stretch to – the Cadbury range – wow! Every time I went to the egg farm my eyes would almost pop out of their sockets and, because of my waywardness, the chocolate bars were soon stuffed in my pockets!

Now I knew that stealing was absolutely wrong and I also knew what it was to have a great big guilty conscience, but that was something I thought I could handle. The days we went to the egg farm were days of high adventure. We rode our bikes along the roads leading to the outskirts of Broadstone, where the farm was situated. We laughed and had such glee on our faces as we declared to each other that we were bandits! Once at the farm it was easy – too easy. One of us would keep look-out while the rest of us stuffed our pockets with sweets. Sometimes we were very bold and actually paid for about two pennies worth of Mojos, while we carried away almost all the Egg Farm stock from the shelves in our pockets.

We never got caught. Maybe the owners suspected us, but they never challenged us about the disappearance of so much stock during those long hot days of the summer holiday. The Egg Farm experience bolstered my confidence as a sneak thief, looking out for opportunities to make a killing.

Of course stealing was wrong! I knew that, but if other people had plenty, did it really matter? Andrew a school-mate, had everything! Well it seemed that way as I gazed around his bedroom. At that time of my life Action Man was the 'in toy'; every schoolboy had an Action Man and the lucky ones had all the best outfits and the accessories. Andrew's bedroom looked like a showroom for Palitoy, the maker of the plastic hero. You name it, from deep-sea diver to space man, Andrew had all the Action Man uni-forms. I, on the other hand, didn't have many and so the only way to get more Action Man uniforms seemed to be by stealing them from Andrew.

Andrew was very trusting, and before long we were best of mates, or so he thought. I would ask him if we could play Action Man and when he said, 'yes', I would visit him after school. His mum would open the door to me, a young tearaway carrying a naked Action Man, and I would rush into the house. We would play for hours in the bedroom and when Andrew's mum shouted that it was time for me to go home, she never seemed to recognise that my Action Man was leaving with a set of clothes, and often with an arsenal that would put 'Rambo' to shame!

The Little Rec

Beside Springdale Infant school there was a small recreation ground that we called the 'Little Rec'. It had swings, a slide, a seesaw and an excellent witches hat that was constantly being damaged, as the bigger kids would somehow take the hat off its pivot at the top. The witches hat became the rigging of a pirate ship for us! We spent hours rocking back and forth and spinning round on that thing. Thankfully, I never came to any harm, although I knew of some kids who had fallen off and broken their arms.

The Little Rec also had a great dirt track path running from the main road right through the middle of the park, turning up a hill and leading to the council's garage, where all the green-keeping equipment was kept. For my seventh birthday I was given a bike, which I loved, and Colin and I would race the other kids in what we called 'Speedway' down the dirt track. The summer months were the best, because as we sped down the dirt track dust would go flying all over the place, and as we skidded to a halt at the end of the racetrack we would be lost in a cloud. We would also stick a piece of card into the spokes of the wheels so that we had an 'authentic' engine sound as we sped along.

The Little Rec became my domain. I had a gang of kids hanging out with me, and most of the time they did what I said. We broke the windows of the council garage, we started small fires, and we'd climb onto the roof of the Wendy house and make a general nuisance of ourselves. Bit by bit, this would filter back to Mr and Mrs Smith. They were very good and although they told me off when it was needed, they also loved me in their correction.

The Little Rec was as I said, a 'paradise' for a little gang leader such as myself; I got up to all sorts of mischief. One summer's day as the holidays became boring, I climbed a tall tree in the park, then Colin and two others from my gang went and telephoned the fire station using the 999 number. Wow, it was something to see a beautiful big red fire engine approach the park! The lights were flashing and the siren blaring as it came to a stop right under my tree. I could have easily got down, but I had to be rescued now and this delighted the gang members as a burly fireman gently helped their leader down the ladder. They took my details and sure enough Mrs Smith asked me about it later that day. I was told not to climb the trees again and never to waste the fire service's time with such pranks. Being told that they could have been rescuing somebody in a real fire rather than wasting their time on us did not, however, sink into my heart at that time. To me it was just a good laugh and after all, I didn't care about anybody else anyway.

At the very top of the park was a little stream that ran alongside the school playing field and eventually went under a fence into a man's back garden. That stream was too big a temptation to resist. Parts of the stream were not too deep and when I had my wellies on I could wade up the stream being sure to keep to the sides so as not to have wet socks. This was like wading up some South American rain forest stream: the trees were so low over the water I would pretend to cut back the undergrowth and make a path for those following me. Using branches from the willow trees, we would swing like Tarzan over the water. Often there

There would be a cracking noise and a splash as a branch gave way and someone ended up in the stream

would be a cracking noise and a splash as a branch gave way and someone ended up in the stream. We would shout and howl as this happened.

All the noise of splashing water and screaming boys attracted the attention of the man who lived in the garden into which the stream flowed. He would come out of his garden through a little gate and bellow at us, reminding us constantly that it was private land and that we were trespassing. I forget his name, but remember that he looked a little like Edward Heath, and seeing his red face explode made it all the more fun. In fact, we would go on raiding parties right up to his garden and poke our heads under the fence where the stream flowed. Sometimes, if we were particularly bold, we would shout obscenities at him as he sat lounging in the sun on his patio. Sometimes, when we encouraged each other to go a step further in devilment, we would throw dirt bombs that would explode all over his immaculate lawns and crash into his prized flower beds. He would run after us, but luckily he was too old and overweight to catch us.

The man complained to Mrs Smith on several occasions, but when I was asked about upsetting the 'nice' man with the beautiful garden living next to the school, I blatantly denied it.

Lying was becoming a habit of mine, which I thought I had mastered quite well. I noticed at home that if I did something wrong and Colin and I were asked about it, if I kept an innocent face and kept calm, Colin would get all flustered and get the blame! This was most entertaining, as Colin would often get all sorts of punishments that I rightly deserved: the halo around my head would shine so brightly as I lied about things increasingly and watched my brother getting punished.

The Building Site

Every boy loves a building site: there is so much with which to meddle and play. There are all those mounds of dirt with hard sods on top – an ammunition dump for kids who want to play war and like throwing dirt bombs at people; brick and wall ties make good boomerangs or Chinese throwing stars; and walls that have just been laid are fun to push over. There are ladders to climb and scaffolding to run along and from which to lob dirt bombs. The games I could play on a building site were endless. When the signs from the construction company went up on the piece of land next to the school, adjoining the Little Rec, it seemed like heaven to a small, naughty boy!

We were told time and time again to stay away, as the lorries rolled into town carrying bricks, sand and planks, etc. building sites are dangerous, they told us – and so they are – but this one was too big a temptation to resist.

We played war for hours: it was great fun throwing dirt bombs at people! If the bomb missed somebody and hit a brick wall, the sand and cement would explode on impact into a cloud of dust, thus making it look a realistic bomb to a small boy. However, if it hit its target, it didn't always explode! An unexploded bomb always hurt, but I didn't care – after all, war had its casualties!

The builders must have got fed up with all the damage we did night after night. After our tea, we would lie in wait for the men to knock off and then we would strike. We'd take our positions in our imaginary trenches and behind the shelled ruins and then, when we were ready, I would yell at the top of my voice 'War' and the bombing would start. To this day I am surprised that none of us ever got seriously hurt as we threw stones, half bricks, in fact anything that came to hand, at one another.

All good things come to an end, or so they say, and our war games on the building site came to an abrupt end one Friday night. We had already had a week of war games, causing much havoc for the builders as they came in each morning. We waited over in the Little Rec and as the builders cleared off for the weekend we closed in like a band of commandos ready to take our positions as before. This time however it all went horribly wrong, terribly wrong, for as we slipped into the half built houses and began to climb the scaffolding, we were suddenly ambushed by a gang of builders who had been hiding.

Their counter-attack worked well, as we were all caught instantaneously and rounded up together as prisoners of war

The roughneck builders must have got so fed up with the vandalism that they had a war strategy of their own! Their counter-attack worked well, as we were all caught instantaneously and rounded up together as prisoners of war.

Unfortunately for me, they soon realised that I was the commander of the small, defeated band. After a few questions were answered, six of the other boys, along with myself, were flung into the back of the pick-up lorry that had doubled back to fool us. Under guard, we were all marched down the drive of the Smiths' home in great humiliation and shame. The builders didn't mince their words as they brought the charges of damage and havoc caused by our war games, which must have been very embarrassing to Mr and Mrs Smith. They pacified the builders, who were threatening to call the police, by promising to tell us off and to make sure we wouldn't be playing war again on the building site. The builders left, and not long afterwards, so did my mates, leaving me to face the music!

Fire

I remember that during the winter Mrs Smith would make a real fire using chopped wood and coal in the lounge fire grate. Mr Smith would chop up the firewood skilfully with an axe, and I would stand for hours bagging the wood with him on cold Saturday afternoons. He never said much at those times, apart from the fact that he considered it his duty to look after his aunties at Wimborne and his mother, who lived at Blandford, by providing firewood for them.

Whenever Mrs Smith built a fire in the lounge grate, I would ask to light it and she would allow me to do the honours. She would tell me that I was allowed to do this, firstly, because she was supervising me and secondly, because she hoped that I would never go anywhere and start fires on my own. She meant well, but an unhealthy interest in fire-making had already been ignited deep within me and no amount of warnings about the danger of matches would deter me in my quest to explore the way of fire.

One day, when everyone was out of the house, I discovered where the matches were hidden. I would often poke my face into cupboards and drawers once the coast was clear. In the kitchen there was a tall larder cupboard above the fridge, with lots of shelves filled with Tupperware and cake tins, etc. This cupboard was out of bounds, but there comes a time when all children ask the question 'why?' Having asked myself that question, and knowing the coast was clear, I decided to investigate the forbidden place. Among things that were not that interesting to a boy – unless he is into cake making – I found, on the second shelf, a plain cardboard packet with about five brand new matchboxes inside it.

Now, this was a big discovery for a boy like me. Once I knew where the matches were kept the sky was the limit for my experimentation with fire.

I had watched Mr Smith in his garden shed take a strong-smelling purple liquid from a large metal container with a little tap fixed at the bottom. He called this purple liquid 'paraffin', and I noticed that he would put some of it in a heater in his large cold garage and it burned. I also noted that things marked 'flammable' burned well. I had gained an understanding, without letting on or giving any cause for suspicion, and I knew that if I waited, the time would come when I could have lots of fun. I knew that it was wrong; I also knew that it was highly dangerous, but there was a compelling desire to do my own thing.

I would often wait until Mrs Smith went out or was busy in the house and also until Colin was out of the way. I didn't trust him and knew that, under pressure, he would crack and tell the truth, and that would never do. I must have drained that massive barrel of paraffin over the next few weeks. I loved going into that musty old shed and stealing away with a tissue soaked in paraffin, ready to ignite behind the shed at the bottom of the garden. It was amazing that I never set the shed alight with my experiments. A stray match in the store shed would have sent the roof flying, as the paraffin barrel would have exploded along with all the other bottles marked 'flammable'.

Andrew was fascinated by the tales of my paraffin experiments and asked me to take some matches up to his house. I had managed to steal a whole box of matches, which was very risky, as Mrs Smith was still in the house. I got on my bike and cycled all the way up the road as fast as I could to Andrew's house. Alongside Andrew's house was a plot of land that had once had a home upon it. The house was long gone, but the foundations and the cellar remained and were filled with stagnant water. This was another magnet, drawing boys like me to its unfathomable depths.

Andrew and I quickly went onto the 'jungle' plot and found some tall grass growing up the fence of an adjoining house and garden shed. All it took was just one match. I can remember the fear and exhilaration as Andrew and I ran from the inferno that threatened to burn the shed down and spread to the house. We crouched down in the undergrowth, hidden from the frantic house owners and neighbours who had sprung into action in a bid to extinguish the fierce flames. As they began to empty the pool of stagnant water with buckets, which they repeatedly carried to the scene of the fire, we

We could hear the sirens of the fire engines getting louder and louder as the appliances sped up the road

could hear the sirens of the fire engines getting louder and louder as the appliances sped up the road. It was a good job we were hiding – to be seen at this time would have incriminated us as the arsonists.

I knew, once again, I had done a silly and very dangerous thing. The possibility of people burning to death didn't really cross my mind, but the buzz of starting a fire sure felt good, and was something that I would repeat many times in the years to follow.

Smoking

Mr Smith used to smoke and had done so since he was a young man. His Aunt Mary, who lived at Wimborne, would also light up a cigarette in front of young eyes. I

would watch as grown-ups lit up and inhaled that
delicious-looking smoke. I would hold my breath as the
smoke disappeared from view. where it went I didn't
know, but it always came out again, and that was a trick
that I really wanted to learn. Once, when Mr Smith
became ill and was off work, he decided to quit the habit.
Whether for financial reasons or health reasons I can't
remember, but I do remember him constantly chewing
gum or sucking mints afterwards. Because Mr Smith had
quit smoking I was not going to have a chance to experiment with his tobacco, and so I had to bide my time.

My big break came when I was nearly nine years old.
A couple of mates and I had gone into Broadstone on our
bikes, and as I rode along I noticed that it was bin day and
people had put their bins out. As I came near to the end
of the road, a man came out of his gate, saw the bins, put
his bag down and went back into his garden to fetch his
bin. I quickly stopped by the man's open bag, which had
been left on the pavement, and there, for all to see, was a
brand new packet of cigarettes. I couldn't help myself (as
I later discovered a good opportunist thief is always on
the look-out for something to steal). Like a bird of prey
swooping for the kill, my little hand dived into the bag
and seized those cigarettes for myself. Heart beating
wildly, I was off on my bike once more and around the
corner before the man reappeared with his bin! Now I
was going to have some great fun.

I rode to the Little Rec with my two friends and we hid
the packet of cigarettes under a brick, alongside the wall
of the council garage. cycling home, I knew we were on a
mission. I had to get hold of some matches – for cigarettes
without matches would be no fun at all. We all had a
drink of squash and then went out into the garden. I doubled back into the house and again, at great risk of being

caught red-handed by Mrs Smith, set out to get matches from the tall larder cupboard in the kitchen. Once again, I was lucky and wasn't caught. With the matches shoved down the front of my trousers, I went and found Mrs Smith busy cleaning in the bedrooms. On gaining permission to go back to the Little Rec, we went flying off once more. Lying down in the long grass we each held a cigarette. How big we all thought we looked, how grown up and sophisticated we felt, as we lit up and inhaled the first lungful of deadly smoke. Those first cigarettes were a novelty – in fact, we got through the whole packet of twenty in one afternoon!

Little did I suspect the awful addiction those cigarettes would bring upon me – years of slavery to the cruel taskmaster called Nicotine. It was the start of an addiction that would have me at its mercy for many years and lower me to such depths of indignity as I craved for my nicotine fix. When I had no money for cigarettes, I would make cigars from leaves in the woods. I would use dry blackberry and bramble leaves, crushed and rolled up in public toilet paper, in a bid to feed my smoking habit.

Later, when I was at school, I would steal cigarettes from one of the teachers and have a quick puff in the toilets by the gym. The secret was to steal just one cigarette each night, that way she never caught on that she was feeding my illicit addiction.

I thought I was incredibly grown up when, at the age of 15, I bought myself a pipe! What a sight as people walked past a bench in Poole Park and watched me puffing on a pipe, as if I was some old man sitting in the sun, soaking up the warm rays and fondly remembering some past event.

There was a shop on the corner of a parade of shops near the park that sold papers, sweets and cigarettes of all sorts.

The owner was an older man who was unscrupulous in his business transactions with young kids. Even if you couldn't see over his counter, if you had the money you could have any type of tobacco that you liked. I loved nothing more than buying a nice cigar on a summer's day and then going into the park. Then, when I was seated on a branch of my favourite tree, I would light up, enjoying the mellow flavour and aromatic smell as I smoked my cigar, and watched the day pass by.

I can remember people warning us that if we smoked we would be hooked and also that we could die of lung cancer. However, when you're young and not even a teenager, when you're someone who thinks you have your whole life yet to live, lung cancer is not a consideration. If you get hooked, so what! It's what you enjoy doing, isn't it? And so it was that I became hooked on nicotine. The craving for a cigarette didn't happen overnight, but it did come. So anyone who thinks they can try it and control it, be warned. Thousands today are desperately trying to quit and, through the effort of trying to be free from nicotine, they are now realising the full strength of addiction and its mighty hold on their lives. I pity anyone now who is trying to break free from the power of smoking. I know firsthand the awful feeling of dependence for that cigarette as you wake up. That instinctive reaching for the cigarette as you finish your meal. The anxious feeling if you run out late at night and you know the shops will be shut. My addiction was awful, and only the power of God could set me free.

> *My addiction was awful, and only the power of God could set me free*

As I remember those early days at Broadstone, I think of happy times: times of fun and laughter, when the sun seemed to shine all the time. However, clouds were on the horizon that would blot out the sun, leaving me in the cold shade – a darkness that would block out the warmth and light for years to come.

3

BOARDING SCHOOL

One beautiful summer's day, our Persian social worker came to visit us. She brought with her, as an offering to gain our friendship, some used postage stamps from Persia. She then took Colin and me for a walk, individually, in the back garden for a chat. She began to explain to me that Mr and Mrs Smith had not been feeling so well of late; also, that they were extremely tired and that it would help them if we changed school. She then asked me if I would like to go for a drive with her, Mrs Smith and Colin into the New Forest to see a new school that we could go to if we liked.

I wonder now just how much choice we had, if any. Knowing the social services of the time, I guess we really had no choice! But she was good at her job, and she soon told us all the good things about the school as we sped along the dual carriageway.

The school was a preparatory boarding school for the very young up to secondary education age. It had originally been a girls' school, but had relocated some years before to this amazing manor house. The old house was rich in history, having served as a hideout for Loyalists to the Crown during the English civil war. The owner had bravely hidden soldiers fleeing from Oliver Cromwell's men and had paid for it with her life, being caught, tried and sentenced to death. Because of the house's bloody history, it was reputed to have been haunted by those executed by the Roundheads under Oliver Cromwell. I never saw any apparitions of the ghostly kind, but on many occasions I had fearful nightmares and felt an icy cold, evil, almost suffocating presence in the small hours as I ventured to use the bathroom. There was a secret closet there, in which the cavaliers had hidden before being caught by the Roundheads.

> *I had fearful nightmares and felt an icy cold, evil, almost suffocating presence*

The house had three floors. On the ground floor were reception rooms, staff rooms, classrooms and common rooms. The other two floors were filled with dormitories and bathrooms. The grounds were extensive, covering acres, with paddocks and beautiful rhododendrons bushing out along the borders of what seemed like a jungle to small children. There were the remains of a Second World War air raid shelter that we played in for hours and hours. The roof had long gone, but we ran along the top of the walls, leaping across the gaps and narrowly avoiding injury as we barely made it. Then there was the plantation adjoining the school grounds, and, if you climbed through the hole in the fence, you could walk for what seemed miles.

The school had bike sheds, and an outside swimming pool, which I broke one year by throwing a sharp stone onto the ice on a frosty day. The stone bounced along the ice ripping into the vinyl liner along the side wall. When the ice melted my sin was fully revealed and I had the slipper from the headmaster.

When we rolled up the front drive of the school that first afternoon, the taste of adventure and something new had a great appeal. The headmaster seemed strict, but said all the right things to lure two boys into saying 'Yes' to his school. We were given a guided tour around the school – all the best bits of course! We were shown a dormitory with only three beds in it, and a bathroom with one bath, which we later learned was for staff only.

Later that day, as our social worker drove us home, she asked what we thought of the school. Both Colin and I chirped up from the back of the car that it looked great. Then she asked us whether, if she could arrange it, which would probably take some doing, we would like to go there? When we said yes, we didn't realise that it would be the start of a new chapter in our lives. In fact, our life with the Smiths was coming to a close, and Colin and I would not be together for much longer. If I had known then, the pain I was about to go through in the next few months, I would have never agreed to go. Upon reflection, I now realise that it would have been impossible for Colin or me to stay with Terry and Sally Smith, for our behaviour had become so bad that it was the final nail in the coffin.

The summer holidays came and went very quickly that year. There was much excitement as our new school uniforms were bought and Mrs Smith sewed our names onto everything, socks and all.

The September term began and I realised that with it I had started a whole new life. Once Mr and Mrs Smith had gone, Colin and I were taken upstairs to our dormitory, and we then realised that the room we were now placed in was not the one we had seen earlier on our first visit! This dormitory had eight beds in it and we were suddenly exposed to public school life.

Miss Collins the matron – or 'Colley', as everyone, staff and children alike, affectionately knew her – began to go through our possessions. She went through everything, like a trained customs officer, with nothing escaping her beady eye. My penknife was taken instantly, much to my displeasure. At the interview the headmaster had assured me that I could have my penknife with me – after all, this had been a deciding factor for me in going to the school in the first place! Colley had a heart of gold; and she always wore a spotlessly clean white coat. She had a

> *She went through everything, like a trained customs officer*

red face and a mop of white hair to match the brilliance of her coat. She was strict and took no prisoners, but had a way about her that won the children's hearts.

Discipline can be unpleasant for anyone: after all, we all want to do our own thing. Yet with discipline there is a great degree of security, and security brings peace. Small children away from home need peace, especially for those first few days. Colley introduced us to the other six boys sharing the dormitory. They were all old hands, at seven to nine years of age, and they looked at us with suspicion, probably wondering how long we would last the new regime! We were marched down to the dining room for supper – a glass of milk and some cake – then swiftly marched back up to the bathroom, where we lined up to use the loos and to brush our teeth.

Once we were in bed, Colley read out the riot act. Potential offenders were warned of the dreaded 'Colley's jobs' that took place on Saturday mornings for anyone who stepped over the line. Those jobs were feared and hated by all the children: cleaning, dusting, mopping and polishing, etc, while all the other children were having free time and playing elsewhere around the school grounds.

As soon as the lights went off the interrogation started. 'What's your name?' 'Where do you come from?' 'What does your dad do?' I began to answer the questions, hoping to give an acceptable reply, when suddenly the door flung open and the door frame was filled with the awesome sight of Colley! I said she was strict, so, first night or not, we all ended up doing Colley's jobs that first Saturday morning!

The first term went very quickly. We didn't get a chance to feel homesick, because so much was happening all the time. Every day I was making new friends, literally from the four corners of the earth. There were children whose parents were government officials and the like, from china, Africa and even Papua New Guinea.

Sadness

I had settled down well at school and enjoyed the routine of public school life. However, like all the children, I looked forward to going home for the holidays, sleeping in my own bed, having all my toys around me, playing in my old stomping grounds, and being loved and cuddled by Mr and Mrs Smith. The Autumn term had flown by and now we were going home for the Christmas holiday.

Like all children, I loved the excitement of Christmas, and I wrote out the list to Father Christmas of toys I wanted, unaware that another big change was going to occur in my life. Those few days before Christmas had an air of menace about them. Mr and Mrs Smith seemed tense, and I had an uneasy feeling that all was not well, yet I could not put my finger upon what. Christmas Day came, and as usual we leapt out of bed and ripped open the packages that Father Christmas had left the night before. After lunch, Mrs Smith took me to one side and she had tears welling up in her eyes as she told me that Colin and I would be going to see our real mother on Boxing Day.

I had never felt comfortable with my real mum or with her common-law husband. In fact there was something sinister about him that gave me the creeps. I remember protesting that I didn't want to go, but Mrs Smith explained that we had to, even though she didn't seem happy about it herself.

That Boxing Day was the worst day of my young life. It was the day I felt that my heart had been torn out and I wanted to die. We had breakfast, and afterwards I was surprised to see Mr Smith putting many of our belongings, such as toys and bags of our clothes, into the car. Why did we need so much for one day? The journey was quiet. By now the tension was getting unbearable, and when we pulled up outside my real mum's house both Mr and Mrs Smith had eyes that were filling with tears.

They knocked on the door and, although my mum greeted us with a big smile, I felt an awful sense of foreboding: something was dreadfully wrong. I felt nervous, like an animal lining up outside the slaughterhouse, knowing and sensing something is wrong, but being unable to do anything about it.

> *That Boxing Day was the worst day of my young life. it was the day I felt that my heart had been torn out and I wanted to die*

The Smiths kissed us and hugged us and then they were suddenly gone. If I had known then what I would discover hours later, I wouldn't have let go of them. In fact, I would have refused to even enter the house. Mum tried to make an effort and her 'husband' smiled at us, but through his smile I felt unwelcome and a nuisance to him. After a bit of lunch, which I didn't feel like eating, and with a lump in my throat, I asked the fateful question 'When are we going home?' Mum said, 'Didn't the Smiths tell you that you aren't going home?' Everything spun around in my mind. The feeling of foreboding now made sense. Tears began to flow down my face as I said I wanted to go home. Her 'husband' began to get cross with me and shouted at me, accusing me of being ungrateful. I cried all the more and he shouted all the more. They put me in the front room on my own and so I cried all afternoon. I was desperate to go back to the Smiths' house, my home, and yet it was impossible.

That night someone came to baby-sit Colin and me as Mum and her husband were going out drinking. As we lay on put-up beds in the front room, I sobbed and sobbed. Colin was quiet. I don't think he realised the full horror of what had happened to us. I was still crying in the early hours as they came home. I remember the fear deep inside my quivering heart as he began to swear at mum and hit her because it was all her fault that Colin and I were in his house. He shouted and screamed all sorts of obscenities at mum, Colin and me. The tears flowed and flowed into the next day. In fact, when morning came, I was in such an emotional state with puffy eyes, that mum called the social services out as an emergency. Two ladies came to see us about mid-morning. I was so badly affected by the events of the past day that I couldn't even talk to them coherently. It was obvious to these young women that a big mistake had been made and that they were dealing with a young boy who was absolutely broken-hearted. They told me that, for all sorts of reasons, I could not go back to the Smiths, but I wasn't listening to them because of all my sobbing. Colin had also heard the shouting the night before, and his story corroborated mine. Hearing all this made the women social workers concerned for our safety. They had a chat with mum, and within minutes all our kit was packed again, and this time we were in the car heading for the Bournemouth Observation and Assessment Centre.

> *As we lay on put-up beds in the front room, I sobbed and sobbed. Colin was quiet. I don't think he realised the full horror of what had happened to us*

That place was a nightmare. I thought I had problems! Kids were brought to that place from the types of situation that luridly fill the front pages of the tabloids. The staff were neither loving nor caring. Now, as the extent of abuse in children's homes throughout the seventies is being revealed, I can well believe what the people who went through those homes as children are saying. Thankfully, those days at the O and A Centre were short-lived, as the next school term came round quickly.

Once back at school, I felt, initially, a sense of relief: at least I was in familiar surroundings again and that helped a little. But the sight of the other kids hugging and waving goodbye to their parents until they would meet again, was all too much for me. That night I laid my head down to sleep, but sleep was far from me as my mind was awash with all sorts of disturbing things: Who would love me now? Who would look after me? Where do I go from here? Such thoughts, and the memories of being at Broadstone with the Smiths, churned my tattered emotions and the tears began to flow. I kept as quiet as I could, as a river of salty tears flowed upon my pillow, which was soon saturated. I struggled with my breathing, as anxiety engulfed my mind and I felt wave after wave of panic buffet me like breakers upon the rocks. Yet I dared not make a sound, lest anyone else should know I had been crying. I already had the shame of having no one in the world and no home in the world. I could not add to that the indignity of a nine-year old boy sobbing – that would have been too much.

For about a week, I hid the pain that was tearing me apart inside. All I wanted was to be accepted, to be loved, to be hugged and feel wanted. Was that too much to ask? Now, many years later, I often ask myself how many children are feeling the same thing?

The night-time routine of crying myself to sleep was making me insecure and scared to do anything in case I would be rejected for the slightest thing. One night it all got too much and I felt as if I wanted to die – and that's something no one should feel, especially a young child of nine. I felt that having those feelings of grief and sorrow were wrong and that somehow I was letting the side down in having such emotions. Yet enough was enough, I had to be with somebody.

I climbed stealthily out of my bed and remember to this day the chill I felt on my wet pyjama top as I crept out of the dormitory and climbed the stairs to Colley's room. I was terrified of being rejected and told off by Colley, but the inner pain was too much and I had to be with someone. I knocked on her door and she came out immediately, as she was still up. She took one look at my tear-stained face and I broke down sobbing uncontrollably, burying my face in her plump side. 'There, there,' she said. Colley had probably said the same thing to hundreds of weeping children over her years as a matron, yet for me at this hour of my greatest need, it was all I wanted to hear. Colley cuddled me, and as she sat me on her lap, spoke to me softly, explaining that everything would work out all right in the end. The next few months found me at Colley's door a few more times, but she was patient with me and helped me overcome my life's greatest crisis.

The half-term holiday was rapidly approaching, and Colin and I had nowhere to go. Whether the social services had mixed up the holiday dates I am not sure, but the O and A Centre was not available, as it was full up with other poor children suffering probably much more than us. Colley and Miss Sparrow, an older lady who helped with the evening duties of bathing and bedding down the young boarders, came to the rescue. It was decided that Colin would go with Miss Sparrow to her sister's house, a farm in Devon, and I would stay with Colley.

Colley lived opposite the school, in a fine modern house with her two older sisters, neither of whom had ever married. The sisters obviously knew about my situation and went overboard to spoil me, which I remember actually enjoying. Although Colley put on a tough exterior, she, too, made me more than welcome. I remember going with Colley up to Malvern, which seemed miles and miles away from the school, to visit Miss Hunt, the old headmistress of the school who had retired before I had first enrolled as a pupil. She was kind and gentle and I instantly took to her. The two ladies took me to Malvern common and I flew a kite that they had bought for me.

I remember one night in particular, feeling great anxiety gripping me, and having nightmares about my uncertain future. Such was my fear of the unknown and distress about the present that I wet the bed. I was very embarrassed about it when it was discovered the following morning. These two women were great. The sheets were off and in the washing basket and new clean linen placed upon my bed even before I had time to say sorry.

By the time the half-term break was over, I was getting used to the idea that I no longer had a regular family or a place that I could call home.

As I grew used to my new situation, I got on with life – after all, what else could I do at 10 years of age? Schooldays at Moyles Court were fun. The regime was pretty tough, but the hours spent in those lovely grounds made all the hours behind a desk doing maths worth it.

I was made the school postman – that was a fantastic job, because I got to ride the famous post bike, an old rickety thing that was held together by the rust. But more than that, I collected the mail from the office and distributed it to all the boarders. They all used to hold their breath as I walked into the room, every eye looking at me, hoping I would call out their name and hold out an envelope sent from home.

Every lunchtime, I would go to see to the school secretary, who would give me the outgoing mail. It was normally a bundle of brown envelopes, probably invoices to all the parents, held together with a thick elastic band. These letters were then put in a canvas satchel with a strap that went over my shoulder. I then had to cycle a mile down the road to the nearest post box. The highlight of the trip would be to ride over the ford in the stream running very close to the school. If the water level was high, it would come up to the pedals, and that was good fun. If it were low tide, I would cycle at full speed into the water and delight in the spray that was always refreshing during those long hot summer days.

Having the responsibility of being the postman was like being a Pony Express rider; if the weather was bad the mail still had to get through. Come floods or snow, the mail was always posted and always delivered faithfully to the children. Having the job was helpful, because nobody wrote to me and I guess no one thought to ask why I never had my name read out when the post was delivered. They probably all thought I had put my letters to one side, or had already read them because, after all, I was the postman.

Mount Everest

I spent much of my free time discovering the beautiful surrounds of the school. The jungle of undergrowth was amazing and there was no end to the trees I could climb. I remember the tallest tree by a climbing frame, a massive red cedar that was known to all as 'Mount Everest'. Only experienced tree climbers were allowed to climb that lofty peak, and then it was under strict supervision of a member of staff. You had to wear PE shorts and plimsolls, and also a jumper, because it got windy at the top!

First-termers were not allowed to climb Mount Everest, but from the moment I was told all the rules of the climb, the challenge rose in me. Only the best kids assailed those heights and I was determined to be among the elite number that had become legendary in the history of the school.

The first Saturday morning of the next term, I got my chance to become one of the few who could boast of climbing Mount Everest. I got permission and was inspected for dress and equipment before the ascent. A small group of children gathered at the bottom of the tree. The group normally grew in size the higher you climbed – the possibility of a fall probably generated more interest than a victor at the peak! The first branches were the worst: the gardener had cut away the lower limbs so younger children had no chance at all of starting the epic climb. In fact, if you could not master the first part of the tree, it was considered that you wouldn't have a chance later, and the climb would be abandoned in great embarrassment. I struggled and gritted my teeth as I tackled the first few feet. With grazed knees and scratched hands I looked up, and was single-minded in my quest to conquer Mount Everest. After what seemed to be all morning, I began to gain confidence and gain height as well. Soon I could see all over the grounds of the school, and the people below were like little ants scurrying around. The final few feet took my breath away as I realised that I had made it. Yes, I was 10 years old and I had climbed Mount Everest!

The final few feet took my breath away as I realised that I had made it. Yes, I was 10 years old and I had climbed Mount Everest

The feeling of elation was hard to contain as I started the climb downwards. Yet contain it I must, because, in fact, the descent was worse than the ascent. My legs were by now scratched and bloodied, but as I dropped to the ground to the cheer of the crowd I wasn't concerned. After all, I was the returning hero, I was the conqueror and, for the moment, I had the limelight – and boy, didn't it feel good even if it lasted for only a few minutes!

Stupid Things

I did some daft and stupid things from time to time. One night during the summer term, when most of the younger children had gone in to be bathed and put to bed, I was on my own, as the other children of my age group were mainly girls and had already gone to the common room to play some game. I found my way into the old bike shed, which housed all the bikes belonging to the schoolchildren. It was beginning to get dark and the last warm rays of the setting sun settled on the tin roof, causing it to remain warm inside.

I discovered, in the fading light, as I was searching along one of the shelves reserved for the school caretaker, a tube of glue used for repairing punctures. On taking the lid off, and probably because the air wasn't ventilated well in the shed, I got a whiff of the glue's powerful, intoxicating vapours. These smells seemed to make me feel as if I was floating, yes even flying – a sensation I had never known before – and I actually enjoyed it.

Being something of an experimentalist, and with my head spinning, I rolled up a piece of scrap card and poured the glue down it. Then holding it instinctively as a cigarette, I had my first experience of 'getting high'.

Thinking about it now, it was no small miracle that I didn't die. Many times, young people experiment with glue and drugs and find – to the heartache of all concerned – that the first time is their last time – which is very sad.

I was completely 'out of it'. Talk about 'Lucy in the Sky with Diamonds'! I was rolling around on the dusty shed floor, high as a kite. I was totally intoxicated by the strong glue fumes, and when I finally managed to leave the shed, I collapsed again by the side of the swimming pool. Thankfully nobody saw me from the window and it was a secret that went with me when I left the school later. That was my first experience of being high, and it gave me a temporary release from the inner pain and emptiness that expressed its hunger more deeply each day.

Boarding school was the place where I discovered that girls were definitely different to boys, and could prove to be very interesting! Nancy was a gorgeous blonde, who was at that age when she, as I did, thought it very grown up to kiss. Although relationships at a preparatory school were very few and far between, Nancy and I struck up a friendship. It all started when our eyes met over the desks of a boring French lesson. Maybe it was the amorous language or the way I pronounced *'Je t'aime'*, but she smiled at me and that was enough for me to write a love letter to her. Letters were exchanged across the classroom all afternoon, and when school was over and we had an hour of free time to fill before tea, we met up. The grounds afforded lots of shelter and so Nancy and I met up behind

> *It all started when our eyes met over the desks of a boring French lesson. Maybe it was the amorous language or the way I pronounced 'Je t'aime'*

one of the rhododendron bushes. The only problem was that she brought her best friend Vicky with her! That, although an embarrassment at first, soon proved to be a blessing for young love, as Vicky seemed to know all there was to know about kissing. Nancy and I kissed, but, according to Vicky, we got it all wrong. Apparently we had to use our tongues like the French people did. Well we used our tongues and discovered that was far more interesting. Then the moment came when we had to get more intimate: 'Show me yours and I'll show you mine' . . . the rest is censored!

Colley and the other night matrons didn't seem to notice that some of us boys were growing up. Stuart and I were developing a keen interest in the girls. Stuart was a year older than me and encouraged one particular girl to come to our two-bed dormitory and give us a striptease. The girl was from an African state, and was highly developed for 12 years of age, and the sight of her nude form did even more to fuel my interest in girls.

School was where I had my first proper girlfriend, Hazel Bodmin. Hazel was full of fun and, although not a stunner like Nancy, she was great to be with, and she liked nothing more than to take me into the locker room by the gym to sample the delights of continental kissing. Thankfully, it never went any further than that, but I'll always remember her as my first proper girlfriend.

I could write forever about my days at boarding school, but, once again, the sands of time were running out for me there. I was getting older, and so had to embark upon the next part of my journey into adulthood. This part of the journey would take me out of the beautiful surrounds of Moyles Court School and take me to Somerset, where my next school was located.

4

CHILDREN'S HOME KID

We had to go somewhere for the holidays. Kind as Colley and Miss Sparrow were, the temporary arrangement of half term was never repeated. By now we had a new social worker, another lady who said she knew all about boys. I very much doubt she did, for she never seemed to take any of my feelings into consideration when plans were drawn up for my life. This social worker took Colin and me to a children's home in Poole, Dorset. This was a residential home which housed a maximum of twenty-one children. We called the officer in charge Auntie Jenny. A deputy and other staff assisted her. The staff worked shifts, coming on in twos at 2 p.m. every afternoon and working through by sleeping over on site till 2 p.m. the next day. Auntie Jenny always seemed to be around, and even if she was off duty you could usually find her in the office with a mountain of paperwork.

The home was originally situated in an older property not far from Poole Park, but the building fell into disrepair and I guess the council decided it was time for a purpose-built home. This was good in the sense of having amenities, but it did nothing for character, and the place, although modern and called a children's home, was definitely not a home in any normal sense of the word. We were welcomed as soon as we arrived and introduced to the staff on duty. Auntie Jenny gave us the guided tour and took us to a bedroom upstairs with three beds in it. By now I didn't mind dormitory life: in fact, I had got used to it, and a room to myself would have seemed strange. They felt it best to keep Colin and me together in a bid to help us settle in as quickly as possible. The other children were still at school and so we were able to familiarise ourselves with the layout of the home quietly. Then, one by one, the regular 'inmates' began to return from their day at school. First, the loud 'special needs' children who came by taxi (no wonder the social services say they have no money!), then the other children turned up, and once again we went through the interrogation process. This time it was nowhere near as bad as the boarding school experience, because these kids knew the system. They were like old lags, who taught us the ropes and what to watch out for. Nearly all of them had a horrific story of abuse and family break up to tell. We were all in the same boat, and so it was survival of the fittest. In this home no one was going to stop and listen to a sob story, for we all had one to tell.

Nearly all of them had a horrific story of abuse and family break up to tell

The children's home was a place of great discovery! A place where I learned much more about girls and sex, a place where I learned to shoplift, a place where I first got drunk and did many other crazy things. Incredibly I did all these things right under the noses of the staff, and, for the most part, they never confronted me or stopped me growing up the way that I had decided to. Inside me was a great emptiness, a feeling that there had to be more, a

need to be loved and wanted. All these internal feelings
fuelled the fire of the things that I would experience in the
coming few years.

Girls!

I had been at the home for only a few nights. Each
evening we would have to go through the bath-time rit-
ual and, after scrubbing-up, we could go downstairs to
watch telly, read, or listen to records in the games room.
Joss, a girl who was much older than me, was very friendly. She invited me to listen to records with her in the
games room and I, thinking she looked good and was
being nice to me, went along. The staff would be upstairs
supervising the bath times and also putting the very
young kids to bed. This left the whole ground floor wide
open to anything, from kids smoking in the lounge (the
designated smoking room for the 16+) to kids like me
indulging in the forbidden fruits of the flesh. Joss soon
had me dancing with her and before long we were kissing. The skills I had picked up from Nancy and Hazel
paid off, and I passed as an experienced lover to Joss, who
had been with boys before. Things soon got hot and we
decided to meet later that night. Once I had gone to bed,
the time seemed to take forever for Joss to come upstairs
at her allotted bedtime. Her room was just across the corridor from my door and was set back a couple of feet from
the main corridor. A gentle tapping on my door signalled
she was ready to meet me.

What a risk we took, as we stood kissing against the wall
of the children's home corridor. To be caught would have
brought great trouble upon us, and probably all the staff of
the home as well. As we stood in a passionate embrace, I
lost my virginity. I am not proud of the way it happened,

because it was the start of what would be a stronghold in my life, as I went from one partner to the next. Sex was easy at the home, and it seemed free at the time, but I paid for it later because it was the start of a slippery road that led to the depths of pornography, as I grabbed all the sex I could, in a bid to fill the great empty space in my life. I experimented with sex in many of the rooms of the home, and also in places in the grounds. The staff never seemed to see what was happening, and if they did, they chose not to say anything in order to have a quiet life.

Crime

Ben, an older lad who was about 15, used to take me to the shops in Parkstone on Saturday afternoons. He was bold and knew what he was doing. He was confident in his skills of shoplifting. The first time he took me with him stealing, we went into the Co-op supermarket. When we had walked around the shop he led me back out. I was puzzled, because he had told me he was going in there for chocolate, but he hadn't bought anything. When I questioned him about it he just laughed and showed me the contents of his pockets. Bar after bar of Cadbury's chocolate and other expensive delights appeared. My bulging eyes nearly popped out of their sockets. Ben told me never to tell anybody, and better still, promised to teach me all he knew. A real Fagin, he showed me how to look out for store detectives and store operatives, how to look like a proper shopper and not a teenage thief, how to fill your pockets with the best stuff and get it through the door without being caught.

Shane, a friend from the home, was of the same breed as me. He also wanted the good things and, not having the cash to pay for it, had the same option – go without, or steal it. Shane and I became the perfect crime partnership. We spent hours walking through the shopping centre in the centre of Poole acquiring all sorts of goodies our pocket money could never afford. The difficult problem wasn't in the stealing, but the explaining of how we found such bargains and bought so much with the rationed pocket money Dorset County Council gave us! We had all sorts of scams to make extra money.

One of the best, which always worked, was our begging trick. I would go up to a kindly-looking man or woman and with a pained, troubled look, I would ask for money, explaining that my brother was ill and I had no money to phone home. In those days, it would be two or five pence, and I had only to approach a few people in the crowded shopping mall and my income was supplemented very nicely.

The other easy cash trick was to fish for it! Yes, that's right, fishing. Not the type where you sit by a pond, but the kind where you roll up your sleeve and, in front of hundreds of people, drop a comb into the fishpond in the middle of the shopping centre. The pond had fish in it, but also the bottom was covered in money, coins thrown in for different charities. This trick took a certain cheek, as the whole thing had to look as if you had genuinely dropped something into the water. Then, in front of everyone, you had to fish out what you had 'accidentally' dropped, but along with the comb or whatever was dropped you also palmed a few of the coins from the bottom of the pond! The trick normally worked well and added a great deal extra to our pocket money. But when the arcade managers swept the coins into the centre of the pond things got more difficult. I remember being chased out of that arcade with a soaked and dripping arm on more than one occasion by security guards who spotted us illegally fishing!

One place that had a magnetic draw on me and the other baby bandits was the amusement arcade on Poole Quay. This arcade was alive with flashing lights, the sounds of sirens and bells going off continually, with pop music blaring in the background. This amusement arcade was the place to increase my cash: a get-rich-quick haven that was guaranteed, with one simple tool of the bandit's trade, the '*Star Wars* card'. *Star Wars* was the film of my early teens, and, of course, part of the obligatory mer-chandise was the bubble gum with collectors cards filled with images from the blockbuster of the decade.

What has a *Star Wars* card to do with getting money from the arcade? Simple – the arcade boasted some of the finest cascade machines I had ever set my eyes upon. For the uninitiated, cascade machines are the gambling machines with moving shelves that are heavily laden with coins – some with those high currency coins, the fifty-pence pieces of the early eighties. The shelves would go back and forth and the object of the gamble would be to drop a coin, usually a two-pence or five-pence piece, down a slot. If dropped at the right time, the coin would help to push money over the edge of the shelves as they went back and forth. Normally there were two shelves, and the honest punter, who would be lured by greed and what looked like easy money, would often lose his cash. At the start of the day, the arcade operators carefully placed the cash on the shelves, and it would take a lot of dropped coins to budge that build-up of overhanging coins. But the machine had one serious flaw, and we knew it.

The glass front where the coins were dropped upon the shelves had a gap that was just big enough for a *Star Wars* card to be inserted. Once correctly inserted, the *Star Wars* card did its job, sending coins cascading over the first shelf onto the second shelf. By now, the card would be back in your pocket out of sight, and as the money began to pour into the winning tray you had to look innocent and full of excitement, as you appeared to be a big winner! That *Star Wars* card trick earned me a small fortune.

It wasn't all success though, as I can still remember the pain as a size ten boot made sudden contact with my rear! I was slung out of the back door of that arcade a number of times and given a few 'lifetime' bans! The arcade was a good place for an opportunist thief as well. Shane and I would wait until a tourist – and there would be plenty of those – came into the arcade, and had placed their bags on the ground. Then, when the gaming machines gripped them, we struck by stealing anything that looked like it was worth a few pounds. Unfortunately, much of what we stole ended up at the bottom of the quay because we didn't have a 'fence' (somebody to sell stolen items to) at that time.

We had to make up a good excuse to go to town because any trip to town without money would look suspicious. So we became 'train spotters'! The railway line went right through the top of Poole High Street and, with level-crossing gates and a footbridge over the track, train spotting was the perfect excuse to get access to the shopping centre. Woolworths was only a few shops down from the level crossing and a prime target. Most of the staff at Woolworths were older, and the style and layout of the store afforded good cover for even an amateur shoplifter. I was into collecting model cars, as most boys of my age were, and Woolworths did an excellent line in replica model motorcycles! Those models were a piece of cake to take out of the presentation boxes and stuff into the coat pocket of my parka. By the end of the summer holiday, I had a whole collection of brightly coloured miniature motorcycles, and not only that, but a great boldness in my shoplifting skills.

Tesco was another shop like Woolworths, an easy hit for me. I guess I was a competent shoplifter in my teens, and Tesco was just another place to get what I wanted. I had acquired a taste for whisky and so would 'pick up' a small bottle every day. I would take my whisky into the Tesco in-store restaurant and brazenly pour some of it out into my coca-cola! I also regularly 'picked up' my new clothes from Tesco's home and wear department. My friend Shane would go one step further. Rather than do his washing, which we all had to do ourselves in the home, he would pick a whole change of clothes, changing his socks and underpants and leaving the dirty ones in the changing room!

The Undertakers and Juvenile Court

The walk into town always had shorts cuts, and one of those was behind some shops on the approach to Poole town centre. As we walked past the back of the different businesses, I would always slow down at the undertakers! Those gleaming hearses and sparkling limousines attracted my attention. What really intrigued me were the wooden boxes with flowers on top! Now one of those with wheels screwed to the bottom would make a fantastic go-cart! One Saturday morning, as we walked past the undertaker's garage, we noticed there was nobody about. Shane, Colin and I looked at each other, all knowing what the others were thinking. In a flash we were in the garage, hearts beating wildly, knowing this place was the place of the dead. Half expecting to bump into a zombie, we edged our way from the garage into the interior rooms. We only opened one door, probably because we were scared of being caught. That was the door to the chapel of rest! Shane and Colin went in, and as they passed through the doorway I gave them both a great big push that sent them crashing into an open coffin that had a rather grey-faced gentleman inside! I howled with delight, but they screamed in terror as they came face to face with their first corpse. I quickly slammed the chapel of rest door shut from the outside and held it tight, as Shane and Colin, who were desperate to get out, tried to pull the door open from the inside. My fun came to a swift end as I heard the undertaker, alerted by all the noise, shouting up the pathway at us. We ran as fast as we could from that place. I was laughing so much though, I could hardly run at all and the other two threatened to beat me up because of what I had just done to them.

> *What really intrigued me were the wooden boxes with flowers on top. Now one of those with wheels screwed to the bottom would make a fantastic go-cart!*

We never did get the go-cart, but we did end those summer holidays in big trouble! Because we were all stealing and shoplifting together, sooner or later we were going to be caught. It came one afternoon as Auntie Jenny called us one by one into her office. The sight of this angry woman and her threats soon made me come clean about my criminal exploits, just as the others had already done before me. As we confessed to all we had been doing, the catalogue of crimes grew larger by the minute. Auntie Jenny had no choice but to call the police. We sat in the lounge looking glumly at the floor and ceiling, no one daring to speak, waiting for the police to arrive. When they finally came we all had to go one by one back into the office and make a statement. Most of the kids got off with a caution, but Shane, Colin and I had done so much we were charged and summoned to Poole Juvenile Court.

I don't think I really understood just how serious it all was. I will never forget this, my first court appearance. The chairman of the Juvenile Court, Mr Robertson, had a rounded balding head and a massive nose that looked like Concord in flight! The more I looked at him the more I laughed, to his obvious annoyance. Then, when he challenged me on violating the place of the dead and asked me why I did it, I couldn't contain my laughter. When I finally pulled myself together and told him I wanted to steal a coffin to make a go-cart, he hit the roof. I was given a severe warning but, thankfully, discharged. Shane, however, wasn't as lucky as Colin and me, for he was sentenced to six months in borstal.

The Staff

On the whole, I think that the staff at the children's home were good people. Some seemed more caring than others and some seemed more terrifying. Uncle Harry was one that none of us messed with. He was in his forties and had worked in other places before he had settled into residential children's care. He did so only because his wife was the officer in charge. Uncle Harry was not a soft touch and always put on a hard-man image to staff and children alike. He would be outspoken and didn't care who he offended. He was not afraid of anything or anybody. He was a person who had done it all and liked everyone to know it! He would brag to us about the years he served in the Army doing his National Service.

Meal times were an ordeal, and a living nightmare for any kid who hated to eat their vegetables. To be fair, the home always served up good food – not always what we wanted – but, nonetheless, good wholesome food using diet sheets that had been approved by the county council.

The dining room was large enough to have four tables, where six people could sit comfortably around each one. Once the two members of staff on duty had served the food, they would come and join us as we ate our meals. But Uncle Harry, who said he was brought up hard, couldn't stand the sight of one pea left on a plate. He would be furious if he saw a helping of cabbage or a brussels sprout uneaten. He would be the enforcer! No one was going to waste food – not on his tour of duty. He would come up to the side of some poor quivering child and, taking their fork by force, would spear a sprout. Then, holding the fork about an inch from their eyes, he would say, 'If you don't eat this I'll ram it down your throat!' What child is going to argue with such bullying? Uncle Harry meant what he said. If force were needed, he would use it, and not minimum force either. I saw him use force on others, and there were times when he was happy to use it on me as well.

'If you don't eat this I'll ram it down your throat!'

You never knew where you were with Uncle Harry. Just when you thought you knew him, something would happen and you realised how wrong you were. If we were pillow-fighting in our dormitory, you could guarantee it would be Uncle Harry who would stealthily creep upon us like a commando and crack our heads together.

The man instilled fear in most of us, and that fear caused us to creep around him. We would ask the staff who was going to be on the next shift, and would shiver as if someone had walked over our graves when they said Auntie Jenny and Uncle Harry. I can remember times when Auntie Jenny would get the wrong end of the stick as she waded in to sort out disputes among the children. As the innocent party protested the truth, Uncle Harry would come in heavy-handed and 'quieten' any resistance. Even when Uncle Harry had a day off, we would only sigh in relief as his Ford Cortina cruised up the drive and away from the children's home. I laugh now as I can hear the petrified warning shouts resounding around the home, as some kid spotted his car returning from a trip out!

The children's home staff were always strict – I guess they had to be – and none of them ever gave in or showed any real affection to any one of us. It was probably forbidden for the staff to really love us and to show it by an occasional hug. But a hug and some loving affection was what we wanted more than anything else in the whole world. Many of us had been rejected, even discarded like surplus property by our parents. All we wanted was love. The county council fulfilled its duty *in loco parentis*, but duty was all it was. The regulations and the system prevented us from starving or even being abused by bad parents. However, it never fulfilled our greatest need, to be loved and to be able to give love.

> *A hug and some loving affection was what we wanted more than anything else in the whole world*

Uncle Owen came to the home one Sunday afternoon. He was a small man with blonde hair, a big bushy blonde moustache and a great big smile that won your heart immediately. Uncle Owen was a radical. I didn't realise it until years later, but he was a challenge to the system that was cold and unfeeling. He wanted us to laugh, to be able to talk freely about the pain inside and to be able to enjoy ourselves. For hours he would talk to us and write poems about us that would make us laugh and smile. He would champion our causes and didn't flinch in the face of Uncle Harry. Uncle Harry couldn't stand this ray of hope and sunshine that had suddenly lit the dark recesses of the home. The two of them were never on duty together. I think if that had ever happened there would have been sparks and bloodshed, for Uncle Owen would not have put up with Uncle Harry's table manners! Uncle Owen was with us for the summer holiday period, and as fast as he came, he went again. We all kept asking questions about Uncle Owen's strange disappearance, and although no official reason was given, one of the lady members of staff told us that there was a conflict of understanding in disciplinary matters concerning the care of children. The bottom line was that Uncle Owen had challenged the hierarchy of the home, his love and forward thinking had threatened their security and so a campaign had been mounted to remove him. Sadly it had been successful.

I met Uncle Owen years later walking down Poole High Street, and when we recognised each other, what a hug we had in front of everyone. He was genuinely pleased that I had survived my time at the home. We never met again, but that one meeting was enough for us both to remember.

There was one member of staff who also sticks clearly in my mind. Auntie Janet was a pretty-faced young woman who I first saw when she came for a job interview one afternoon. She had been to college and was trained for children's care. She impressed the interview board and so she got the job. Auntie Janet seemed different to the others – she didn't smoke, swear or smile at anything smutty. Her father was the minister of the Broadstone United Reformed Church, although she never verbally confessed her faith, which was probably something she was forbidden to do, particularly to young impressionable children. Auntie Janet was quiet and always fair when trying to arbitrate during heated debates among the children. She never lost her cool or shouted like the other staff, and yes, the more I think about it, there was certainly something different about her.

I wonder if she was a Christian? Certainly by the way she lived, I would say today she probably was. I like to think, also, that she prayed for us kids. She would have seen hurting children longing to be loved and accepted. She would have known the Saviour's feelings for children: how he loved them and hugged them, picked them up and blessed them and scolded the disciples when they tried to keep the kids away. Jesus knew the simplistic faith of a child and said, 'Don't stop them! For the kingdom of heaven belongs to such as these', as the kids pushed past the strong ex-fishermen to jump on Jesus' lap.

Years later, at the 1996 Assemblies of God conference, where I was ordained as a minister, I met one of the ladies who had spent her childhood at the home. As my wife and I drank a cup of tea in our chalet at Bognor Regis, we listened as she told us of others from the home who had been saved by the grace of God. I can still see her face now, smiling as we remembered those painful, hurting days of our youth. The joy of Jesus was indeed her strength, for she, too, could write a book about being set free from the kingdom of darkness. We talked of Auntie Janet and wondered whether she prayed for us all. If she had prayed for us, as we guessed she did, then she, too, would rejoice with us. For out of all of those kids at the home during our time there, five are now Christians and enjoying God's love and healing power in their lives. We hugged each other as we parted, praising God that we had come through and now possessed the greatest life in the world through Jesus Christ, who loved us and gave himself for us.

5

THE KINGOM OF DARKNESS

First Impressions

The day I went with a social worker to view the new boarding school, it rained. Colin was not with us, as it was decided by the social services that he needed to be placed in a special educational needs school. There was such a school in Poole, so Colin remained at the children's home. Maybe the rain was an omen that I wouldn't be happy at this next school. As the car sped through the Somerset roads, we approached Yeovil, and the social worker, a man whose name I can't remember, began to give me a briefing about trying to create a good impression to all the people I would soon be meeting. During the last few miles of the trip I felt sick. I had always suffered from travel sickness, but maybe it was more than the motion of the car – maybe it was also a feeling of dread as I was once again facing the unknown.

I was breathing in deeply as we turned off the main road into the school grounds. A farm building on one side of the road and an old church on the other, made the entrance to the school look mysterious yet impressive. The school had great big gates that, once passed through, gave view to a fabulous-looking manor house with ivy growing up the walls, giving an aged but magnificent appearance. The drive circled round past the front porch creating a grass roundabout island with a flagpole in the middle. That certainly impressed me, but what really grabbed me was the Sea Venom fighter jet parked on the grass and the two anti-aircraft gun emplacements. I didn't want to speak to any teachers now: instead I wanted to explore all the exciting things at the front of the school. My social worker was firm and insisted that we get on with the business of meeting the headmaster.

The doorbell was rung, and after what seemed ages, a tall and somewhat overweight man with incredibly bushy eyebrows appeared. This was the headmaster, and he soon made us feel welcome as he shook our hands and asked us to follow him. We went through the front door, a privilege that I was seldom allowed in the future, as it was forbidden for pupils to use it. The main hall was quite awe-inspiring, the prominent feature being a grand wooden staircase with elaborate carvings. The walls were filled with original paintings of people from the past who had probably lived in the house over the years it had stood.

As we followed the headmaster into his office – a place that I would learn to try to keep out of – we passed a gun case containing all sorts of rifles locked safely away. All these images flashed through my mind and I thought to myself that maybe this wouldn't be such a bad place after all. After a short chat, in which the headmaster spelled out a brief history of the school and its involvement with the Royal Navy through the Sea Cadets, I was asked to do a short test. The questions didn't look official, but I guess they wanted to know how intelligent I was and what they would be taking on!

Once the test was over, the guided tour began. We saw a dormitory, the classrooms, school library, the many playing fields and a large gymnasium. The swimming pool was looking green, but some excuse was given for its strange colour and also a reassurance that it would be ready for use by the time I started at the school!

The tour took a long time and I should have remembered the last tour at Moyles Court when I was only shown the 'best bits' of the school! But the sight of all those guns and the aeroplanes parked on the grass thrilled me and then there was the school's own stream and water mill with a deep pool filled with eels. Even better, it had its own fire station, fully equipped with uniforms and a vintage Dennis fire engine.

This was all too much for a young boy, and so I was hooked! By the time we shook hands with the headmaster and his wife, it had been agreed that I would be starting at the school as a new pupil in the coming Autumn term.

> *This was all too much for a young boy, and so I was hooked!*

September soon came around and once again the car carrying me sped through the Somerset roads. This time my suitcase was in the boot, loaded with my new uniform. The uniform was pretty good for the young boys enrolling at the school – black trousers and an army jumper complete with epaulettes. The girls wore the same jumpers, but had black leather trousers or skirts, which apparently had won an award in the past for the 'most practical school uniform'.

The Lords of Discipline

The school had a system of discipline with much of the authority delegated to older pupils who had three ranks – head boy and head girl, prefects and aides. I was to discover very quickly, to my terror, that these ruling pupils ran the school once the academic day was over. They organised shower times, enforced bedtimes and dished out punishments called 'defaulters' to anyone they chose.

The aides had a small common room not far from the main hall and stairway of the school. Walking past the door of that common room was very risky, as the door would often be slightly ajar and just as you thought you had slipped by unnoticed someone would shout out your name. Once your name was called you had no choice but to obey! The common room door would be promptly shut and torture would be the menu of the day, from crushed hands to red ears and noses.

One day, as I crept along the corridor, I was summoned into the common room and interrogated about something that someone else was supposed to have done. Because my answers were not what they wanted to hear, the five aides in the room ordered me to stand in front of the dartboard. Then, as I stood in absolute terror, they began to play 'Around the Clock'. I begged them to stop, but what was a 12-year-old boy to five young men between seventeen and nineteen? To make matters worse, they demanded that I keep my eyes open. The fear of losing my sight was real and I had a job to control my bladder. Mercifully, my ordeal ended as one of them threw his dart wildly and it missed the board lodging itself deep in my leg below my knee instead! Because the tears started flowing down my cheeks they released me, and although blood oozed from the fresh wound, I counted myself lucky to be alive and to

> *Although blood oozed from the fresh wound, I counted myself lucky to be alive and to come out of that hellhole in one piece*

come out of that hellhole in one piece, as others had suffered much worse at the hands of those cruel bullies.

The school, although good academically, was hopeless at after school supervision. Because of this, I was exposed to all sorts of things no young teenager should face. I became a nasty person as I grew up: uncaring, cold, selfish, filthy-tongued and perverse in many ways. I can't blame my wrongdoings on anyone else: as the Bible clearly says, we all have to give an account for our own lives. Yet I can't help but think that the school had helped turn me into an evil, cold, scheming crook who would go on from that place to bring misery, not only to myself, but also to the lives of many other people.

Although I had quickly picked up many scams, things didn't always go to plan! I will never forget the day a little scheme of mine backfired badly. The school always had afternoon games at least twice a week and, not being keen on cross-country running or wanting to donate a copious supply of blood on the rugby field, I would bunk off with a couple of mates. In the summer, we would go and climb a tall tree at the end of the school grounds. Sitting in the lofty branches, we would enjoy a quiet smoke and watch the other lads doing athletics, sweating in the heat of the day. During the winter, we would slip into the changing rooms after all the other lads, who had stood in the yard for roll call, ran off to the sports event of their choice. As the thundering rumble of football boots on concrete faded away we would laugh at the others playing barbaric games on the frozen rugby pitch, while we lit up our cigarettes in the warmth of the shower room.

On one particular Wednesday afternoon, a visiting rugby team came to play an inter-schools match with a trophy at stake. It was a freezing day and so, as always, we quietly slipped into the changing room area as all the others went to the field to cheer on the home side. We lit up our cigarettes, but were troubled when we heard Mr Shorthand talking to somebody in the yard outside. Once he had gone, we darted into the school library. Although we couldn't smoke in there, at least it was warmer than the freezing rugby pitch!

At the end of the match, as everyone came in from the fields, we slipped out of the library and joined the crowd as if we had been with everyone all the time. It all seemed a perfect plan. It had always worked so well. Suddenly, a cry came from the visiting school team's changing room. A lad had been robbed! Fifteen pounds had been taken from his wallet left in his trouser pocket. Now this had brought great shame upon the school. The headmaster was furious and instructed the 'Lords of Discipline' to seek out the perpetrator of such a scandalous crime.

The head boy immediately made initial inquiries, and by teatime had established that I, along with about six others, was absent from the rugby match. One by one we were summoned to the infamous aides' common room. Trembling, I stood before the head boy and had to give my sorry account of bunking off. The problem for me was that I had actually been in the vicinity of where the cash was stolen. It looked pretty bad for the others and me as we all protested our innocence to a kangaroo court that needed a scapegoat.

The days that followed were an absolute nightmare for a boy of 12. The teachers must have seen something or heard on the grapevine that severe bullying was going on, but nothing was done to protect the weak and vulnerable younger children from the hands of the vicious older pupils. The Lords of Discipline were under increasing pressure to reveal the identity of the thief. The honour of the school was at stake, and if they couldn't produce the culprit by the end of the autumn term, the school's Christmas party was under the threat of cancellation. I can still remember the nights I was interrogated by the prefects. The terror of those nights haunted me for years afterwards. My dormitory was at the end of an ancient wine cellar corridor. To get to the dormitory and the toilet and washbasin area, you had to go through the long dark wine cellar.

In those nights of terror, I would be woken by the sound of many marching hobnailed boots crashing down on the cellar floor, getting louder and louder as they drew closer to the dormitory. With a loud bang the door would be kicked open, almost coming off its hinges. Practically wetting myself with fear as I cowered in bed, the aides and prefects would drag me screaming from my bed. All the other lads in the room knew I was going to get a severe beating, but they were too petrified to raise any objection to the horrific interrogations. I would be thrown against the wash area wall, where they would take turns each night to lead the questioning. I was kicked in the groin so many times, I am amazed that I survived and have been able to experience the joy of being a dad. The sickening pain and the vomiting, as a size ten hobnailed Sea Cadet boot crashed into my testicles, is something I shall never forget.

Night after night, they thought up some new torture to extract a confession from me, just to satisfy the headmaster. They filled a washbasin with water and held my face under the water until I nearly drowned. Then, when I refused to confess to a crime I didn't commit, they would swear at me, holding sharp penknives under my throat. My blood would freeze as they threatened to cut me and slice the flesh off my bones. One night, a cigarette lighter was used to burn the side of my face. As the pain became unbearable I sobbed, but the sound of a pitiful young boy in abject fear didn't move their callous hearts. Once, when they had kept up the torture for a week, the sound of their boots along the corridor didn't wake me. But a starting pistol fired right by my face did. My hearing was impaired for days afterwards, and I had a black grease burn mark down the side of my face. To my despair, not one teacher inquired as to why my face was injured. Not one teacher observed the way I cowered around the grounds and walked in terror in the school building.

> *My blood would freeze as they threatened to cut me and slice the flesh off my bones*

One day, the boy who stole the money revealed himself to me. He was about 16 years old and much bigger than I was, and to protect him he shall remain nameless. He actually boasted to me that he committed the crime and said that I was going to take the blame for him! Early one morning before breakfast he told me to follow him into the exercise yard. As I went through the door he had passed to go outside, he turned on me, placing a well-aimed fist straight in my young face. I was on the floor with blood spurting from a near broken nose and stars before my eyes. He informed me that that was just for starters, unless I confessed to the theft of the fifteen pounds. I hated him for that. The pain was dreadful, but as I picked myself up off the floor, I vowed I would get even with this big bully.

The next day I went to the school fire station and climbed into the driving seat of the vintage fire engine. Stealing the ignition keys, I took them outside and threw them into the bushes. Then, getting a tube of glue, I squirted the adhesive over the seats of the appliance. I let down all the tyres of the fire engine and finally grabbed an axe from inside the cab, which I took round to the science laboratory and sent it crashing through the window. I left the devastation that I had caused in the fire station and went looking for the headmaster. When I found him I asked him if I could have a private word in his ear, to which he agreed. I told him the name of the bully who had punched me and stolen the fifteen pounds, and explained that I had seen that lad messing around in the fire station and that I was worried that he would blame something else on me. The headmaster told me I had done the right thing in going to him and he would keep this information confidential. As I watched him stroll over to the fire station, I knew that my plan was going to work. Sure enough, that very day, the bully's parents were summoned to the school. The lad got a good caning, and by that evening had been expelled. I never saw him again, nor did I want to. None of the younger lads liked him, as he would steal from them. He was a vicious, bullying thug, and I thought that my day's work was in the best interests of all. The beatings stopped from that very day, as everyone quickly learned that the expelled bully was the real culprit.

I should have learned my lesson from the theft of the fifteen pounds about being in the wrong place at the wrong time. But I always seemed to learn the hard way, unfortunately, through my own stupid mistakes and not someone else's. Jack, my school friend, and I decided it would be fun to go into Yeovil one afternoon, rather than going for the obligatory cross-country run. Once we had lined up in PE kit for role call and the directions for the run were given, everyone was off. However, Jack and I went straight back into the changing room and dressed in our weekend clothes; we were going to hit the town! Once dressed, we walked out through the school gates and waited on the main Yeovil road. Presently a car came round the bend and we flagged it down. The couple inside were going into town and were only too pleased to give us a lift.

As Jack and I walked through Yeovil's busy shopping streets, we laughed to each other as we thought of our exhausted schoolmates gasping for air as they completed the cross-country run. We had a cigarette and bought a burger from wimpy – this was the life! Then, as we walked up to the bus stop to see if we could catch a ride back to somewhere near the school, disaster struck. Mr Banton, head of maths at the school, was heading our way down the high street. We turned in our steps and darted into a side street, but it was too late, as he had seen us.

Knowing that we had probably been spotted, and that the punishment for being absent without leave was a caning, we started back to the school. When we got back, Mr Evans met us. He was a hard welshman who delighted in exacting discipline upon wayward boys. He informed us that we were in big trouble and were to report immediately to the headmaster's quarters. Jack and I knew all too well that the cane was going to make an appearance, so we darted up the back stairs to our dormitory. As quick as we could, we pulled on about four pairs of pants each, hoping that the padding would soften the blows from the caning.

Sure enough, we were told to go into the headmaster's lounge and to bend over. One, two, three . . . yes, six times that cane came down across my backside, and although the extra pants helped, the pain was still very real! When the headmaster got his breath back, he told us to go and report back to Mr Evans. We knocked on Mr Evans' door and he bellowed out that we were to enter. Standing in front of him, he ripped into us verbally that we were scum in dishonouring the school by avoiding the cross-country run and then hitching a lift to Yeovil right outside the school gates. Once he had finished the torrent of abuse, he smacked us both in the mouth, and told us if we ever did anything like that again we would be expelled and he would see to it personally that our feet wouldn't touch the ground.

The school was a typical English boarding school, where the men would be trained to sort out their differences like 'gentlemen'! A boy named Harris, a troublemaker who was two years older than me, started a fight with me one day in the wine cellar. I wasn't particularly violent and didn't go looking for fights either, but when this red-haired lad picked on me I wasn't about to let him walk over me, so I stood my ground. In the cramped space of the wine cellar we began to throw punches and instantly a crowd gathered, baying for blood. When a struggle broke out, and it often did, the younger pupils would dash around the school like African messengers shouting out 'Fight, fight'. everyone would stop what they were doing and come to watch what would usually be a good, unofficial, sporting spectacle.

I didn't think that I stood much chance against Harris, as he was older, taller and heavier. But I was holding my own and, to the delight of the onlookers, had drawn blood from the side of his mouth, which enraged him all the more. Such was the frenzied shouting of the spectators that the PE and Science teacher, Mr Thomas, came along and, with his strong, long arms, quickly separated us. 'Follow me', he commanded, as he walked out of the school to the gymnasium. We followed him, and so did a vast crowd of schoolchildren eager to see more action. Once at the gymnasium, we went inside and the door was shut to everyone else: they had to be content with peeping through the windows. Mr Thomas tossed a pair of old boxing gloves to each of us and then told us to get on with it! After a few short rounds, both of us were wiping blood from our sore, bruised noses. By the fifth round we were exhausted, and so the match was declared a draw and we were told to shake hands. I never fought with Harris again after that day. We had developed a respect for each other and, later on, actually stood up for each other in times of conflict.

Sea Cadets

The school prided itself on its Royal Navy connections. the deputy head, Mr Shorthand, was an ex-Royal Navy fitness and drill instructor, and didn't we know it! Every Tuesday afternoon was allocated to the Sea Cadets, something that I had thought sounded good at first, but learned later to dread and loathe. In my eyes, Sea Cadets was just a good excuse for the aides and the teachers, who doubled up as officers, to bully us and make men out of us. They might have meant well, but it was sheer misery, as most of us hated the drills and all the spit and polish that went with it.

Parades were the things I hated most. It meant hours of getting your uniform ironed correctly and for a young lad that was hard work. When I sat spitting and polishing my parade boots, they never seemed to come up to a shine as they were supposed to, and when they finally did shine, some sadistic older boy would normally stand on them just as we lined up for inspection.

On one parade, we were told that Commander Tricky of the Royal Navy would be giving us a General

Inspection. This man apparently organised the drill cere-
mony for Lord Mountbatton's military funeral. He was a
fussy man and everything had to be absolutely perfect.

The drill practice got so boring, and every time I lifted
that old 303 rifle it seemed to get heavier. Until we got the
order 'general salute – present arms' correct, we would
have to keep on doing it. I think it was exhaustion and
nerves fraying due to all the threats of violence if we didn't
perform well that finally made me crack. The drill officer
came up to me in the line and began to bark right in my face
all the horrible things he was going to do to me. This was
the straw that broke the camel's back and before I could
help myself I shouted a load of abuse back to the bullying
officer. That was it! An example had to be made and I was
going to be the cadet who would be publicly disciplined.

I was marched, in disgrace, to the front of the building,
where most of the cadet force were doing different drills
like knot-tying and gun assembly. The Commanding
Officer, Mr Shorthand, was talking to the headmaster, and
when he was informed of my insubordination, adminis-
trated instant discipline by ordering me to run around the
roundabout grass island in front of the school with the
303 rifle held high above my head. This gave the rest of
the school some comic relief. All their eyes were now
upon me, as not many had dared to defy the powers that
be. The gun was too heavy for me and by the time I had
run about four times around the grass roundabout my
energy was completely drained. I stumbled back in front
of the senior officers and the headmaster. This time
enough was enough, I didn't even care if they expelled
me. So, in anger, this 12-year-old boy flung the rifle down
at their feet, shouted an obscenity (too rude for printing!)
and stormed off. Maybe it was because of my age, maybe
because they realised they had pushed this sailor too far,

but to my amazement nobody followed me. By the time I had walked off my anger and returned to the building a few hours later, it was all forgotten by the adults. That night I was the hero of my dormitory as the lads relived the expression on old Shorthand's face as the rifle I had flung in anger came crashing down at his feet!

Sea Cadets also meant lots of sailing on Sherborne Lake. I hated those afternoons of waterborne activities. Sailing was so boring and left me feeling frustrated. We did all the hard work, while the officer would shout out orders like 'go about'. If you didn't respond quickly enough, the voyage became a misery, as the older cadets would hit us and threaten us with more violence once we got back to school.

If sailing was a bad memory, then my rowing escapades were a nightmare! The coxswain would shout out his orders to the poor shipmates that had to row up and down the lake. With blisters on our hands, we sat on the wet seats of the boat and struggled with those huge, heavy oars. When the order was given to 'ship oars' we would have to take them out of the water and hold them upright in the boat. The cold water would run down our arms, soaking our tops and making the time on the water all the more miserable. I don't think any of my schoolmates enjoyed those afternoons. We endured them, longing for the time we would be ordered off the water and told to get on the school bus for the short trip back to the school.

The Kingdom of Darkness

I was unhappy and, like most people living without God, I felt empty inside. At that time I never had any thoughts about God. I guess the spiritual hunger I felt had to be satisfied, but because of my natural tendency to do wrong, I satisfied it not with the love, peace and joy God offers through his son Jesus Christ, but through the dark powers of the occult. The school had all sorts of teenagers boarding, from many different backgrounds. Through such diversity of thinking, occult ideas were given to me.

I would visit the school library and spend hours of my free time reading the books in the supernatural section. I filled my mind with Satanism, which Dennis Wheatley had so freely written about. I read and reread his books, longing to taste the dark powers of Satan myself. I took great pleasure in reading his obligatory warning at the front of each of his books, that 'the occult is of a real and dangerous nature'. I found myself often drawing satanic symbols and designing Ouija boards, using those same ancient occult symbols I had seen in those old library books.

> *The occult is of a real and dangerous nature*

The school was, as I mentioned earlier, right by an old farmhouse and an ancient church with a graveyard. The farmhouse boasted a gruesome relic from the days of the English Civil War. The relic was a human skull, which had belonged to a Theophilus Broome, a supporter of Oliver Cromwell. On being wounded he had escaped the battlefield on his horse and made his way to his family's home, which was the old farmhouse. The wounded soldier was losing blood and his fight for life. With his dying breath he gasped his last request to his sister and onlooking family. He begged them to sever his head from his torso and bury it separately from his body, so that the Royalist men would not take his head and display it impaled on a pole as an example to other sympathisers to

Cromwell's cause. The dying man then uttered a blood-curdling curse upon any who should meddle with his skull or try to bury it with his body. When Theophilus Broome died, the family carried out his dying wishes by severing his head from his body. The body was buried in the churchyard, but the head was placed in a wooden box, which was hidden in the wall above the dining room door in the old farmhouse.

From time to time, people had tried to remove the gruesome skull and bury it in the churchyard, but every time this was attempted something bad would happen to the persons involved. One man actually died while in the process of burying the skull, when a falling roof slate from the church hit him on the head.

The family living in the old farmhouse believed in the curse and, although they talked freely about the skull, they also always treated the whole thing with great respect. Some time before I went to the school, a television reporter and crew went to make a story about the skull. A researcher with the crew picked up the skull and mocked the whole idea of the curse. Later, after filming, the crew went home. The researcher drove in a separate car, but never reached home as he had an accident on the motorway and was killed.

Once, when I went to the old farmhouse with another lad to hear about the skull, the box was lowered down and placed open on a table in the hallway. The telephone rang and the farmer left us while he answered it. Because of its dark and macabre history, I just had to touch the skull. Much to the horror of my friend I placed my hands upon the dark relic of Theophilus' cranium. I didn't feel anything. I should have been scared to delve into the powers of darkness, but, such was my unhealthy interest in the occult, I had lost my in-built fear of what goes bump in the night. All these tales of curses and the undead fuelled my hunger for the supernatural. One Saturday night I went to the churchyard along with three other boys, and when we found the headstone of Theophilus Broome, attempted to hold a séance. We held hands around the headstone and, as we called upon the powers of the spirit world, the wind began to blow in the darkness of the churchyard. The clouds blocking out the light of the moon added to the atmosphere. The headstones formed dark shapes that looked threatening, as if they were figures surrounding us in our morbid quest to contact those long dead. The wind swept around us and, although no one saw or heard anything, I sensed a real and tangible presence of evil that sent a shiver down my spine.

> *We held hands around the headstone and, as we called upon the powers of the spirit world, the wind began to blow in the darkness of the churchyard*

The skull story fascinated me, but it didn't satisfy my lusting for occult power. Dennis Wheatley and other authors had painted this picture in my immature, impressionable mind that there was real power to be had in following the dark lord, Lucifer. I actually believed Satan would reward me with supernatural abilities if I gave myself over to him.

From the moment I saw the tarot cards, I knew that fortune-telling was something I could do. A lad who also had a great interest in the occult brought a deck of tarot cards back to school with him. Some of the boys in our dormitory thought it a laugh, but for me it was more: this was a serious business to investigate. This deck of cards could bring joy or sorrow and even fear to people. I looked upon it as an expression of the power I believed Satan had given me. I stole some money from a tuck box to buy the cards from the lad. Once they were in my hands, I began to call upon Satan, asking him to empower me more than ever. I would read the cards for different people in the school, and they would be amazed as I would explain through the cards their past experiences and what emotions they were feeling at that time. They would gasp as I revealed their future to them.

I enjoyed the power of fortune-telling in the beginning, as it gave me a sense of excitement. But, although I had tasted forbidden dark powers, it didn't satisfy my hungry heart. I read the cards for a few years and learned also to read palms, which was a little more challenging. I really had called on Satan and believed I had the gift for such things in the supernatural. One rainy Saturday afternoon, as I talked with a boy slightly older than myself about my experiences with the occult, he asked me if I had ever tried astral projection. I had read about this eastern practice, but had not yet tried it out. We talked about the benefits of this different kind of supernatural experience and read that Alistair Crowley, the infamous Satanist and mystic, had often practised the out-of-body experience called astral projection.

That was it! I had to add it to my dark repertoire of occult experiences. We slipped up the back staircase to our third-floor dormitory. As we lay on our beds, we meditated for hours on the 'third eye', the one that the mystics say we have. I remember being disappointed, as nothing seemed to happen. It was that afternoon I called on Satan quietly but determinedly and asked him to give me his power.

The dark seed though, had been planted. To my surprise, some nights later in the small hours, I had this incredible experience: an experience over which I didn't seem to have any control. Whether it was a dream or a supernatural reality created by the dark evil forces of satanic deceit I don't know, but the whole astral projection experience was real. Describing it now, years later, all I can say is that there was an inner struggle, where I was almost fighting for breath and freedom, then, suddenly I was liberated from the confines of my physical body. I had this fantastic sensation of flying. The flying I could control and, as I soared upwards and banked, the whole experience seemed real. I had many such out-of-body adventures, where I would be in places where I could see people and hear what they were saying, but somehow they couldn't see me. The concept of flight fascinated me and I enjoyed it as it was happening.

The scary bit was returning to my body. Now that was frightening, as I seemed to return at such a speed that my whole body would jump like a heart patient being resuscitated by electric shock, almost to the point of falling out of the bed! From the moment of asking Satan for the power to project my body on another plane, to the point when I became a Christian, I had many such astral flights. They became a normal part of my life. Although the experiences were both exhilarating and scary at the same time, they never gave me peace or a lasting feeling of satisfaction.

I wish now that someone had taken me to one side at the beginning of my teenage years and told me all that I was looking for could be found in Jesus Christ. Yes, a life given to him in return would be filled with joy and satisfaction that no pen or tongue could fully tell. Alas it was not to be, and so my quest continued in the murky waters of satanic deceit. I was Satan's willing servant and there was much more of his evil to enter me before I would finally see the light of truth that would set me totally free.

To write more about my search for dark powers would only glorify Satan. In this book I have been open and honest in writing it all as it was. This is not to focus your attention upon the Prince of Darkness, but rather to turn your eyes upon the King of Kings and Lord of Lords whose name is Jesus Christ – Jesus Christ who overcame this world, sin and the devil by the mighty power and triumph of his cross.

The things I recollect have now been forgiven and forgotten by God, but I have written them so that you may comprehend how totally lost my soul was and the captivity that a child as young as I found myself in.

Maybe, as you are reading this now, you are thinking of some child you know, for there are many young children who are in the grip of Satan's vice-like claws. As you think of these child captives, take hope in God. The deliverance that he gave me, he can also give to others. Through prayer, you too can see prisoners such as I was gloriously set free.

Drugs and Drink

The child boarders brought back all sorts of contraband from abroad as they returned from their school holidays. Alex, my mate whose dad was working in India, brought back a great selection of cannabis resin. As soon as he saw me, as he carried his bags up the school's back stairs, he began to tell me of his holiday exploits: the drugs, drink and, of course, the sexual conquests.

That night, in the dormitory, a big 'joint' was rolled up and, as we stood smoking it by the window looking at the stars, my head was swimming. Those short periods of being high temporarily obliterated my inner feelings of insecurity and pain. One of the side-effects of cannabis is laughing, and one of the lads, a tall boy called Flanders, was completely gone, buzzing away and out of control, laughing his head off. This was funny, but it soon wore off as one of the teachers who lived in private quarters in the main house came flying up the stairs in his dressing gown, awakened by the raucous laughter.

Thankfully, I leapt a world record jump over three beds, and managed to get under the covers just as the door flew open! The sight of the teacher standing in the doorway soon brought me back down to earth, but Flanders always went too far and, although he had made it back to his bed like the rest of us, he couldn't suppress his laughter. That, and the smell of the drugs, was a give-away. The teacher asked the dorm leader, a lad called Mark who was pretending to be asleep, who had been smoking drugs? Mark, who was pretty convincing as a roused sleeper, pretended that he didn't know what was going on. The teacher was after blood and threatened to put us all on 'defaulters'. This made Flanders finally confess to the teacher, not to smoking drugs, but to the lesser crime of cigarette smoking. The next day Flanders appeared before the headmaster and, after a lecture on the dangers of smoking, received six of the best and was also told that if he was involved in any more escapades with cigarettes he would be expelled.

Smoking was a regular habit for about half the school. It was forbidden but, as the cigarettes were easy to obtain, children as young as twelve, like myself, were hooked. Obtaining dope was a little more difficult, but as long as you were willing to pay, you could buy as much dope as you liked. I didn't have much money, except for the times when I stole it from other people. However, all was not lost, as I had a good friend nicknamed Curly, who not only had finance, but a regular supplier and so was able to feed his drug habit every week. Curly was probably

my best friend at that time and was happy to share his
drugs with me free of charge! The amazing thing was that
Curly's supplier was actually one of the school's full-time
teachers!

Many a weekend was spent lazing around the shower
rooms 'floating' on the effects of 'Black Leb' or 'Moroccan
Gold'. When drugs were not available, the next best thing
we used to slip out of reality was alcohol. Obtaining
booze was a real adventure and there were two main
sources. one was to buy it illegally and smuggle it back
into the school after a day trip to the largest and nearest
town, which was Yeovil: the other was to steal the headmaster's private supply!

The latter was something I got pretty adept at over a
period of a few months. The headmaster's office, the
place I had my first interview, doubled up as a private
dining room. Among the antique furniture was a side-
board laden with a full decanter of burgundy. Jack, who
was a good friend, and I, discovered the burgundy one
day by chance when we were asked to take, unaccompa-
nied, some boxes of books, to the headmaster's office. We
both drank a mouthful from the decanter. The deep red
liquid burned and glowed as it flowed into our mouths.
We looked at one another with big smiles and purposed
to go back later for more. Jack and I would slip into the
office, one at a time, over the next few days sipping from
the crystal decanter while the other one would stand
guard outside the door in the main hall of the school.

The problem we soon faced was that our little well of
Burgundy was rapidly running dry! And we also faced
the inevitable – our crime would be found out! Two
schoolboys, when posed with such a problem, came up
with the perfect solution. We would pour water into the
decanter and drop some colouring crystals, stolen from

the science laboratory, into the water. It actually worked! I never heard a word about the water that was miraculously turned into Burgundy!

Once you get a taste for drugs, and particularly alcohol, you get this deep hunger to feed the habit. This normally leads to heartache, because sooner or later you have to cross the line of what is right to get what you desperately need. Jack and I faced another problem – our Burgundy supply was no longer available and we both wanted a drink. Jack had recently been in the headmaster's private living quarters, situated on the second floor of the main house, for a caning. While the cane was coming down across his bottom he was gazing straight at a fabulous drinks cabinet. The sight of all

> *Sooner or later you have to cross the line of what is right to get what you desperately need*

those bottles helped ease the pain of the thrashing, and the seeds of temptation were sown.

Somehow, we had to get access to the headmaster's quarters while he was out of the way. Now, every Tuesday morning the headmaster and his wife would treat themselves to a shopping trip for about half a day in Yeovil – that would be the time to get to the drinks cabinet without being caught. The plan came together quickly, as we realised that the school sick bay was part of the headmaster's quarters. The sick bay was, in fact, only a small room with a large window looking out onto an internal yard in the school complex. The room boasted two beds, with little else. The best yet was that the only access was down a little flight of steps through the headmaster's hallway inside his quarters. That was it, we would somehow get into the sick bay and wait for the couple to go out shopping in Yeovil.

Monday morning came and, feeling nervous after the morning break, I went to find matron in her office on the ground floor. Stepping into her office and trying to look convincing as someone who had just vomited, I complained of being sick. I couldn't believe it – it actually worked. This hardened matron took one look at me and marched me up to see the headmaster's wife. She was a hard one to crack. after many questions and taking my temperature she finally allowed me access to the sick bay. Lying in the fresh linen and enjoying the escape from a boring history lesson, I smiled to myself, knowing that the first part of the mission was accomplished and successful. During Monday night, there was a disturbance at the headmaster's door. Jack, in his pyjamas, was almost crying to the headmaster that he had been sick in one of the toilets and wanted to have something for it. The headmaster, who was hopeless in such matters, called for his wife. She finally came, moaning about the late hour and this time said that maybe it was a bug going around the school. Jack was promptly placed in the sick bay, with a bowl by his bed. Then everyone went back to sleep. The next day was hard, as we both had to justify our being in the sick bay. We should have been nominated for an 'Oscar' for our performance, as it worked!

The headmaster's wife told us that if we needed anything we would have to go down the main staircase – that was normally strictly forbidden – and see the school secretary in her office for help.

It seemed to take an eternity for them to go, but finally they went. When we heard them go through the main doors we knew it was party time! What a time we had as we drank from the different bottles of wines and spirits, lying on the headmaster's bed and watching his colour television.

To have been caught would have meant expulsion that very day, and probably six of the best for good measure. The alcoholic cocktails we were swigging soon began to go to our heads and it was a miracle that we left the room for the sick bay when we did. Jack had some mints, which were hot, but we sucked them anyway in case the headmaster's wife wanted to check our temperatures again and would get wind of the booze on our breath.

We sank into those sick bay beds and chalked up another victory against law and order, and against the headmaster and his wife. We could never repeat that Tuesday morning as they would never have bought the fact that the two boys, who were sick together last time, were sick together again. But we had done it, and the thrill of that, for now, was enough to carry us until we felt the need for the next escapade.

Crime

Every criminal likes to think they have a code of so-called honour! I guess up to that point I had not really stolen much from fellow schoolchildren, but that was all to change at the school as I stretched myself to new limits of shame. When I first enrolled they sent a list of things to bring as a boarder. One such thing was a tuck box, something I had never heard of before. In reality, all it consisted of was a box, strengthened by metal corners and a lid fitted with a padlock for security. Everyone had a tuck box in which they could store valuables such as cameras, cash, jewellery, radios, etc. and also sweets and other edible luxuries. Tuck boxes on the whole meant 'Stay away from my property!' but to the criminal they were a piece of cake to open in such a way that nobody would know until it was too late.

Jack and I were good mates and, not only did we steal the headmaster's drink but we collaborated together to steal from the students as well. I soon lost all my scruples when I knew that these children had very wealthy parents or sponsors. We would particularly go for the Arab students' tuck boxes, as they would normally have lots of money, drink, cigarettes and dirty magazines. Once they had discovered that they had been robbed they were helpless: after all, how can you report stolen what was forbidden in the first place!

Saturday nights were a good time for a hit on the tuck boxes, as most of the older Arabs had been to Yeovil and stocked up well with forbidden pleasures. While they watched videos in their common room, Jack and I would steal down into the cellar corridor. This was, in fact, an old wine cellar, complete with all the old stone shelves. The tuck boxes were normally placed one on each shelf and within easy reach for anyone to get access to them. One of us would keep guard at the end of the cellar, while the other, armed with a screwdriver, would undo the hinges of the lid at the back of the tuck box. It was a fiddly job and difficult while your heart pounded wildly with the fear of being caught. But, as the old motto of the SAS goes, 'Who Dares Wins', and a rich booty, indeed, was found in those tuck boxes.

As the old motto of the SAS goes, 'Who Dares Wins'

Jack and I would be set up for the week, with a bountiful supply of cigarettes. Once the dirty deed had been done, we would go for a walk around the school fields, smoking and swigging Scotch or vodka straight from a bottle stolen from one of our Arab friends. Thankfully, we were never caught, for to be caught would have meant a good kicking from the victims and probably immediate expulsion from the school.

Pornography

It's probably a boy thing, but almost every boy growing up loves to look at the lurid, glossy photos of a pornographic magazine. The pages filled with the exposed flesh of models, some old enough to be their mums, hold an attraction to many lads reaching puberty. I, like many others, found pictures of naked women fascinating. I had seen younger girls with no clothes on, but the women in the pictures were much more interesting. I would gaze upon the images for hours and read the stories of erotica, gasping at the so-called sexual adventures of some men. I learned later in life that sex within marriage is undefiled and part of God's plan for a married couple. In fact, sex is a wonderful wedding gift from heaven for those who are married, but it's only intended for the wedding night onwards! I didn't know that at the time, and so wanted all the sex I could get.

One Saturday morning, as the rain came down, as it often did in that picturesque Somerset hamlet, an older friend asked me if I wanted to see a video. Out of boredom and sensing the excitement in the older lad, I said yes. I followed him and another lad into the video room. The video room was not far from the woodwork room. It had rising staging, so a capacity crowd could squeeze in and watch educational films during Geography lessons. Well this film was a real 'education'! It had been borrowed from one of the Arab boys and was red hot! As the images began to appear on the screen I thought it was a medical film, because of the explicit close-up shots of the human genitalia. It was only when the sound was turned up and I heard the ecstatic moans of the women being filmed that I realised I was watching my first hard-core porno film. As I watched the screen in that dark room, I found the images strangely compelling, although I knew that it wasn't right to observe such things in a voyeuristic way.

Those guilty feelings soon dissipated as I grew older, and pornography had a strong hold on my teenage emotions. Because of pornography, I viewed women as sexual objects of desire. Pornography twisted my own sexuality from what was a normal sex drive in a teenager, to a depraved lusting for sexual conquest. It cheapened women in my understanding, defiling my heart with its dark and dangerous passions that in some men lead to serious crimes against women.

Fire and Lies

One of the most serious crimes a person can commit is arson. Starting fires can lead to devastation and loss of life and carries with it heavy penalties. Monday afternoons saw us lining up outside Mr Mason's classroom for geography lessons. Normally it was boring stuff, like rock formation and the course of rivers, but today it was going to be good, as he had promised us an orienteering field trip in a plantation some miles from the school. The minibus was full of excited kids, keen to be out of the classroom for a bit of fun, even if it was only for the afternoon. Once parked up at the plantation, we were told to split up into pairs and to get on with our map reading exercises.

Mark and I set off together to do our assigned tasks. Once out of the sight of everyone else, Mark pulled up his trouser leg to reveal this fabulous diving knife in a holster strapped to his ankle. I was well impressed as he reached for it and handed it to me. With the sun gleaming on the blade, I wished I had a knife like that. Mark explained that it was pretty good as a throwing knife, and he showed me its flight power as he aimed at a plantation tree. The throw was excellent; the problem was Mark's poor sense of direction, as the knife sped past the tree at supersonic speed and landed in the deep grass behind. Mark was devastated, as he had 'borrowed' it from his dad without asking and now it was lost. We searched for it in the deep grass that was yellow and dry due to the summer's drought. After about ten minutes, and with Mark still despairing, I had a brainwave: we should set fire to the grass and then when it was burned we would find the knife. Mark actually had some matches with him and so in seconds we had set fire to the small area where we had been desperately searching. That was a big mistake! One match ignited that grass instantly and within moments a mighty inferno blazed before us, with flames soaring above us far too large to stomp out with our feet. In a panic, we ran away and stopped to catch our breath. We knew that if we were caught, this would place us both in the most serious trouble. The little patch we had lit had now become very large, with the flames leaping from tree to tree. There was only one thing for it, we would run and find Mr Mason and tell him we had discovered a fire. Once alerted, he told us to shout for all the other children and gather together while he alerted the ranger and the fire service.

Within moments a mighty inferno blazed before us

By the time the first fire engine came into the plantation, many acres, valued at thousands of pounds, had been totally destroyed. All the class helped to fight the blaze: taking off our school jumpers we beat the flames out. Finally it was under control, and as we walked back to the minibus the firemen hailed us as young heroes! Once we returned to the school, I had the cheek to campaign to Mr Mason on behalf of the class that we might seek compensation for our damaged shoes and clothes!

There were suspicions though, and the police came to speak to the headmaster and Mr Mason. We were not interviewed directly by the police, probably because of our young age, but we all had to make written statements in our own handwriting of the events of that Monday afternoon field trip. Mark and I had conspired already to say the same thing and so we got away with what could have been fatal to everyone walking in the plantation that Monday afternoon.

There is so much more I could write about my days at the school. I had grown up quickly: from the age of 11 to 13 I had been on a fast track of discovery. I had now clearly left the innocence of childhood behind, and with a heart that was cold and hard, I faced the world and all it would throw at me. I stole, swore, drank alcohol, smoked, took drugs, slept with girls, loved pornography and practised the dark arts of the occult. The school had certainly been an experience. In fact, for me it was like entering through the gateway into the kingdom of darkness: a kingdom of evil that had taken me captive and would never want to let me go until my whole life was taken over by dark satanic forces.

> *My whole life was taken over by dark satanic forces. Dark forces that would eventually try to destroy me and take my very life*

Dark forces that would eventually try to destroy me and take my very life.

6

GO TO JAIL

I had decided to leave the Somerset boarding school. After spending almost two years there, I had finally had enough of the regime. The social services arranged for me to stay permanently at the children's home. They also secured a place for me at a local secondary school. It was an all boys' school right in the centre of Poole, beside the bus station. The old building was in a poor state of repair and the constant exhaust fumes of heavy traffic had blackened the red brick walls.

It was during the days of the summer holiday before I was due to start at my new school that I had been charged and summoned to appear, at a later date, before Poole Juvenile Court. During the lunch break on my first day at the school, Mrs Clark, my class teacher, asked to see me. She was a lady in her sixties and reminded me of Dame Edna Everedge. Although she was a strict lady and had high standards when it came to manners and work performance, she was also kind. She explained to me that she knew all about my upcoming court appearance, and reassured me that if I behaved myself in her lessons she would give a good report of me to the court.

The days seemed to go quickly at secondary school. I wasn't that happy there, but then I probably wasn't going to be happy at any school. I enjoyed my art lessons and would take great satisfaction in painting watercolours. The art room was upstairs, above some storerooms, right by the side of Poole bus station. The art teacher was a strange sort of man who seemed to be a magnet for all the other teachers. They would come up to his small class office and drink tea with him, discussing all their problems, I guess. There was never a lesson when he didn't have a visitor to entertain. We just got on with whatever we wanted to do. Some painted, some carved objects out of lumps of white plaster, some just sat and read, while others would sit in the corner and tattoo themselves with the India ink and needles! When we had an art lesson we were never allowed to go upstairs to the room until the teacher came down to get us. Come rain or shine we always had to wait!

It was while waiting outside the art room that I had my first fight at the school. Every class has its bullies and troublemakers and there were a few in mine! There were three lads who all came from the same neighbourhood and they seemed to be on a mission to make the rest of the class miserable. They would punch and kick other lads and steal their lunch money and cigarettes if they had any. Not a single day would go by without them ganging up on someone.

One particular day, they decided to pick on me outside the art room. One of the terrible three was the big mouth. He would usually wind people up and, once someone retaliated in self-defence, the other two would come muscling in. This lad started accusing me of something or other and I wasn't having it. He

I put my school bag and coat down and began to put my fists up. That was it! The class became like a pack of bloodhounds baying for action

then began to push me around, hoping for a response. He sure got one, as I put my school bag and coat down and began to put my fists up. That was it! The class became like a pack of bloodhounds baying for action.

There was no question of my stepping down, I had the honour of my name to defend now. Within seconds we were grappling with each other. I felt a sharp pain in my leg as one of the other bullies kicked me for good measure. I knew I had to carry on and so forgot about the other two and went for the first lad with all I had. I landed a full fist straight into his nose, instantly bringing him blood and pain. His guard was down and so I continued to punch his face as hard as I could. The other bullies realised they had got more than they had bargained for, but out of loyalty to their friend they dragged me off him just as the art teacher appeared. That was a close call! From that time on, I was never bullied by those three lads again, for I had won their respect and the admiration of the other lads.

Maths was one subject I loathed. I was hopeless with fractions and divisions, along with the other lads in my class, and so the maths teacher despaired of us! He was from Liverpool and football mad. He often told us that we would never be any good at maths, so we might as well all go out and play football! And we did, running and shouting on the sports pitch during maths lessons to the envy of all the other classes. The days it rained we would go over to the public library and spend our time in the reference section. Sitting in the library during maths lessons was fun, but I did have a feeling of being cheated. After all, the maths teacher was head of year and should have made a determined effort to get us enjoying our sums and being confident to enter the adult world with at least an elementary understanding of arithmetic.

One day, as we went into the classroom, we found him with his face in his hands doubled over his desk openly crying. It was the day millions around the world wept, as the news reports came through that John Lennon had been murdered. The teacher was a Liverpudlian in his forties, and the Beatles were everything to him. Now someone had shot down one of his heroes on a New York street. We never did any maths that day, as our teacher gave us a history lesson on the world-renowned 'Fab Four' instead.

Special Fostering

One day, Auntie Jenny, the officer in charge at the children's home called me into her office and chatted to me about special fostering. I had already told my social worker that I felt that I needed to be out of the children's home after the Juvenile Court incident and, knowing how I was feeling, the social services decided to place me in a special foster home. This 'new breed' of carers did it professionally and were paid for their services! My social worker took me one evening to a home not too far away from the children's home. The couple, Brian and Jane, together with their son and daughter welcomed me that night. They went overboard in making me feel at home and before I knew it I was agreeing to leave the children's home to live with them. It only took a few weeks to organise my new residence, which was strange for the bureaucracy of the social services!

On the first night in my new home, I couldn't help wondering if I had made a bad mistake! Jane had cooked tea for everybody, but because I was late home I had to sit in the dining room and eat on my own. I enjoyed my meal and once I had finished, I rose and went to the sink to wash up my plate and cutlery. A simple task done, I went to go upstairs to my room, when all of a sudden Jane came out of the lounge, where she had been sitting quietly with the others and inspected the kitchen. In doing the washing up I had left a few soap bubbles on the draining board. That was it! All hell broke lose as she ranted at me about keeping the house tidy. The noise brought Brian into the kitchen and to be fair he defended me as a 16-year-old boy who had at least appreciated the meal and had made the effort to wash up. Startled by the response of Jane, I went to my room and stayed out of sight for the rest of the evening. I knew then that I wasn't going to get on with Jane. She was a lady who suffered a great deal of pain with her back, and because of these spinal problems she was very irritable with almost everyone in the house throughout the day. I don't mind people having a shout – after all, as the television advert says, 'Its good to talk!' I could put up with a good portion of 'tongue pie' from Jane, but those long periods of sulky, heavy and resentful atmospheres were awful.

They wondered why I never wanted to be with them. They asked why I never ate with them, why I didn't want to go shopping with them and so on. It was because of Jane. I learned to hate her and, when she used to scream out verbal abuse at me, I'd wish she would drop dead. Brian would try to pacify her, but it was no use. If I watched the television with them and got up to use the toilet, she would pull herself out of her chair in pain and reshuffle the cushions on the couch, even though she knew I would be returning shortly!

When she used to scream out verbal abuse at me, I'd wish she would drop dead

The special foster home was supposed to support me,
to care for me and give me the confidence I needed as I
was entering young adulthood. Living with this family
was absolute misery for me, and so I stayed out late from
the home, filling my evenings with casual sex, drinking
and committing crimes.

School was rapidly coming to an end, and as part of a
national initiative we were all offered 'Work Experience'.
As I scanned down the list of local tradesmen who were
willing to have a schoolchild for a week's experience of
their particular trade, my eyes fell upon 'Dewhurst the
Master Butchers'. I knew as soon as I saw the word
'Butchers' that it was for me. Once I had applied, the
wheels were set in motion and I found myself reporting to
Mr Clay, the shop manager, early one Monday morning.

The smell of a butcher's shop is unique – a sweet
aroma of flesh and blood mixed with the distinct smell of
sawdust that always covered the tiled floor. The butchers
were all reasonably young, and as I could make a good
brew of tea I fitted in instantly. They taught me how to
present the pies in the chilled cabinet, how to slice ham
and corned beef so thin that you could read the paper
through it. I learned how to sharpen the big steak knives
with a butcher's steel and how to grind a boning knife
blade so sharp it would split a hair. This was far better
than being in school!

The hours were long and I got no pay, but the reward
of job satisfaction was immense. Everyday I grasped
some new angle of this traditional man's trade, from cutting the carcasses down to making burgers and sausages.
I felt so proud when I stood dressed in a pristine pressed
white butcher's coat with a striped apron and sporting a
butcher's boater hat. There I was behind the counter,
actually serving the great British public.

Mr Clay was pretty strict, but we got on very well, as I was always keen to learn and better myself. The others were a wealth of information, not of the meat kind, but on wine, women and song! I would stand there listening for ages as they told me all sorts of things about life that I had never heard before. My work experience soon came to an end, but because I had excelled in the short time I was there, the district manager promised me a job at the Poole shop as soon as I left school! That was something to be proud of because, out of a class of thirty, I was the only lad who left school with a good job to go to. I really didn't care about my forthcoming exams any more, not once I knew I was going to be a butcher earning £63.00 a week!

I left school and started at Dewhurst the butchers, in Poole High Street, as a full-time trainee butcher. I continued to impress the district manager so much that he enrolled me on a college course every Wednesday at Bournemouth, for the Institute of Meat. I enjoyed the course and passed my exams. I loved the job. I enjoyed all the other aspects of my life, but I still wasn't happy. Deep down, I was empty. How that was possible, I didn't know then. After all, my days were full of activities – some legitimate, some illegitimate. But as a friend of mine once said, 'You can have a full life, but without Jesus, it's not life to the full!'[4]

'You can have a full life, but without Jesus, it's not life to the full!'

Poole Speedway

Although I was working, I kept in contact with Colin and Shane, who were both still at the children's home. Most evenings we would be up to trouble of one sort or another. I certainly preferred their company to Brian and Jane's! I'm not sure who had the original idea, but we decided together one night to go to the speedway stadium and try our luck on the clubhouse and bar attached to the racetrack.

So as not to arouse Brian and Jane's suspicions, I went to bed as normal that night, setting my alarm clock for 2 a.m. When the alarm went off, just a few hours later, I quietly rose from my bed, got dressed in dark clothes and put a pair of black leather gloves and a torch in my jacket pocket. I reached under the bed for my claw hammer and stuck it in my belt. Then, holding my breath, I eased the window open and climbed out onto the porch roof. Closing the window almost shut, I jumped to the ground. The soft front lawn broke my fall and I landed with a gentle thud. Then it was a brisk walk to meet Colin and Shane in the car park of the speedway stadium. Walking along the quiet road into Poole town centre, I lit up a cigarette and couldn't help thinking, with crooked pride, that I was such a professional thief!

Once at the car park, we made our plan. We would climb over a wall and drop down into the track area of the stadium. From there, we would break an entry into the bar area via the toilet blocks that joined the spectator area to the club and bar complex. Like commandos blacked out for covert action, we set our plan into motion. Seconds later and out of breath, we were hiding in the shadows of the spectator seats. The external door to the toilets would somehow have to be opened if our plans were to go any further. Using the hammer and a screwdriver that Shane had brought, we soon crudely chiselled away enough wood to jemmy open the lock with the claw of the hammer. With the sound of splintering wood and then a crack as the door flew open under force, we were in!

The corridor led to the toilet block. we had to get into the toilets to reach our objective – the bar that we hoped would be filled with cash, cigarettes and bottles of spirits. We were one door down and two more to go. The second door was easy: I sat on the floor of the corridor, back against the wall and both feet at the bottom of the door. As I applied the pressure of all my bodyweight against the poorly-manufactured internal door, it gave way almost instantly. My brute force had made a large cat flap and we were through. In the toilets we realised that the next internal door could well be alarmed. With this in mind, we chiselled the lock away using the screwdriver and hammer as before. Once the carpentry was over, we were ready. It was going to be a quick hit: every man for himself, grabbing what he could and getting out before the alarm attracted the attention of the police.

I gave the door a powerful kick and it flew open immediately. Dashing to the bar, we began to grab what we could. To our disgust and disappointment the cash till was empty, the drawer open, but no money to be found. I turned instead to the shelves filled with all the different packets of cigarettes. Taking a carrier bag from my pocket I literally filled it to the top with cigarettes. At least I had got something, but now the fear of being caught made me want to get out of the place as fast as I could.

Running for the toilet door, I noticed the headlights of a car approaching the club from the front car park. I knew it – they had a silent alarm! The others saw the lights as well, and followed me as we dashed through the broken doors and leapt out into the starry night again, fleeing the scene as we ran across the speedway track and over the far side boundary fence.

My heart beating wildly, I ran down the walkway running along the main railway line into Poole station. We crouched in the darkness by the footbridge and quickly divided the spoil. Not much, just about twenty packets of cigarettes each and a few quart bottles of vodka and Scotch. We agreed to split up and meet the next night, and with that, we slipped away separately into the shadows of the coming dawn.

I was able to sell the stolen goods quickly to the guys with whom I was working. They were happy with cut-price cigarettes and booze, so I gained a little money from my night job!

Although the cash incentive wasn't much, the idea of hitting the speedway stadium a second time did appeal to me. I needed the buzz that only a criminal knows as he commits a crime; the excitement and rush of adrenaline as I entered into the arena of dishonesty. The kicks I got out of burglary and other crimes gave me a fix that, although temporary, somehow eased the inner pain and emptiness of my life.

Later, as I explained my plans to Colin and Shane, they found the prospect of a second hit just as exciting as I did – after all, the stadium probably hadn't fixed the doors yet, and they really wouldn't expect burglars to strike twice in two days, surely? We executed our plan exactly as we had the night before. The outer door hadn't been fixed properly: it was just held shut with a piece of wood screwed as a crude latch. inside, the only door repaired was the third door leading directly into the bar. Again, no money, but the cigarettes had been restocked, so we filled our bags again and grabbed a few quart bottles of spirits for good measure and then, once again, we stole away into the night.

The next day I met with Shane. Colin was unable to meet us, so we had a MacDonald's and talked about what crime we would embark on that night. Shane asked whether I had seen the massive Scotch bottle on the side of the bar with coins and five-pound notes in. The bottle was being filled for some charity, and now Shane was suggesting we go back and steal it. The idea seemed good. We wouldn't have to split the proceeds three ways, but two, as Colin wasn't with us. I had a gut feeling that something bad might happen, but Shane kept saying, 'Third time lucky!'

I was feeling tired after the other two nights of breaking and entering, so this time I got out of the house quietly and walked to the nearest telephone box. In those days, you would still find a dirty, foul-smelling directory sitting on the shelf. Looking up a taxi firm, I called one out and waited for the car to pick me up. The taxi arrived and, stupidly, I asked the driver to drop me off at the stadium. The driver, on being paid, drove off. I was early now, but, lighting up a cigarette, I walked over to the dark shadows of the car park and waited. After what seemed ages, a figure appeared out of the darkness – Shane – smiling and ready for action.

Once again, we vaulted over the fence and made our way through the three doors that led to our little Aladdin's cave. Dashing into the bar for the third time, I knew then, deep down inside, that this was not going to be a lucky hit! Just as I picked up the bottle, which was incredibly heavy, tyres screeched to a halt just outside the front of the club. I could see the flashing blue lights of the police cars, and I realised that now was a good time to get out, quick!

Tyres screeched to a halt just outside the front of the club. I could see the flashing blue lights of the police cars

Refusing to give up the bottle filled with cash, I picked it up and we both ran, as before, over the speedway track to the far side of the stadium. Running along the footpath to make our escape from the now pursuing police officers, we approached the footbridge, and I was horrified to see policemen running towards us – we were trapped! With nothing to lose, I ran at one of the officers, who tackled me to the floor. As I went flying, the bottle fell from my arms and smashed onto the tarmac, sending almost two hundred pounds worth of change in every direction. The policemen were furious, as they had to pick up every penny. Later it would be used as evidence against us!

The arresting officers cautioned us immediately and then forcefully marched us over the footbridge to a waiting police transit van on the main road. Sitting inside the police van, a feeling of sickness came upon me as we drove through the dark streets of Poole to the police station.

I had been in trouble before, but now I knew this was the big time; this time it was going to be tough. After I had been presented to the charge sergeant and all my personal effects had been stripped from me and signed for, I was led to an empty cell. Sleep refused to come, although I tried to lie down on the thin mattress and shut my eyes. I just couldn't rest, as thoughts of what would happen next flooded my mind, and I was swamped in anxiety. I tried to shout out through the cell door to Shane, but he was on the other side of the prisoners' exercise yard and couldn't hear me. Somehow, I needed to communicate with him, so that our story would hold up under the experienced scrutiny of the CID investigating officers, who would certainly be interrogating us in the morning.

With the daylight came breakfast, and then the CID. The plain-clothes officers had a whole book of petty

crimes to throw at someone and they chose me as their
fall guy. Basically, if I admitted to petty burglaries, etc.,
they would present them to the court as crimes 'to be
taken into consideration'. If I co-operated with the police,
normally such crimes would go unpunished. The police
would come out as heroes – their crime clear-up rate
would be up! They spent all day trying to pin crimes on
me that I knew I had never committed. However, some of
the scenes of crime they described were my handiwork,
but I wasn't going to tell them that!

We had been caught red-handed and so had to expect
to be charged with that crime. And, although we denied
the first two burglaries at the stadium, they weren't buying it, as it was obvious that the same gang had worked
each night. I was marched down to the charge sergeant
and, in the presence of a social worker, officially charged
with burglary.

Custody

Later that day, I stood with Shane in the dock of Poole
Magistrates Court. The hearing lasted only a few minutes,
but the outcome wasn't good. The chairman of the magistrates ordered that we both be remanded in custody until
the next week, as reports would have to be compiled on us.

There were so many prisoners to be taken to the prison
that day, that an official police van for transporting prisoners was ordered. The cons called this mode of transport
'the horse box' because the van was split up into little
cells designed for about two men each. In reality, four
prisoners were crammed in for the ride from the courthouse to Dorchester prison.

The journey to Dorchester consisted of listening to a
young man who had already been remanded at

Dorchester prison. He took it upon himself to tell us what to expect once we arrived. He warned us about the violence and the homosexuals, who would pounce on younger men in the showers, viciously raping them.

Once the great gates of Dorchester prison had shut on us, we were taken from the custody van and herded like cattle up a ramp and into the prison induction wing. I realised then that this was going to be no picnic! We were told to sit on a bench while the paperwork was completed. Once the induction officer was satisfied that the police had brought the right number of prisoners, he signed for us, and the police left: their job done.

This was going to be no picnic!

When my name was called, I went through into another room with a desk, at which sat two prison officers, whom we all referred to as 'screws'. I was ordered to strip off and so, in red-faced humiliation, I began to remove my clothing hoping that when I had got down to my pants, they would say 'stop', but they didn't! Standing completely naked in front of them, I was further humiliated as they asked me various questions, while other prisoners and officers walked back and forth. Then one of the screws left the desk and stood next to me. He asked me to open my mouth for him, and after that ordered me to touch my toes so that he could check that I had not concealed any drugs about my person. Finally, he allowed me to straighten up and told me to go for the 'sheep dip', which was the obligatory bath for every prisoner inducted into the prison system.

Once bathed, I was thrown a set of prison clothes, complete with the striped 'Ronnie Barker' shirt of *Porridge* fame. The clothes were far too big and I had a job to hold up my trousers. I had other things on my mind at that point, which were far more important. Where were the homosexuals who were waiting to rape me? When could I have a smoke?

I was placed in a small holding cell with two other youths and a couple of older men. We talked about our crimes and were speculating about our possible sentences when the door flew open and tea was served! We each had a stainless steel tray with three compartments on it; a large one for the main dish, some sort of stew and mashed potato, and the others for bread and a type of sponge and custard pudding. The cell went quiet for a moment, then, one by one we complained about the food. One of the older men, a seasoned con, told us we were lucky, as the food was particularly good that day!

Some time later, the door opened again and we were being led into the main prison and up the stairs to the Youth Wing on the second floor. The taunts and shouts of abuse flew from some of the hardened men behind the locked doors. Tobacco was offered as payment if we would prostitute ourselves, and others mocked us calling us 'Baby Burglars'. Eventually, the great barred gate and the secondary locked door of the Youth Wing were opened, and the officer shouted out, 'Two on Sir'. An officer appeared from the wing office. He was wearing a white shirt, which I soon discovered meant he was a senior officer. He ordered us into his office and then went through the regime of the Youth Wing.

It was all pretty straightforward really. Wake up, wash, breakfast. Locked in your cell until lunchtime, out to collect your lunch and then back in the cell until teatime. Out to collect your tea, then, if you're lucky, you get one hour of association time, which basically means watching the telly on the landing, and then it's bedtime! We were supposed to get daily exercise, but that would depend upon the weather! As there were neither coats nor umbrellas, if it was raining, all we could do was to look longingly out through the bars and hope for better weather the next day.

Although I hated every moment of languishing in the Youth Wing of Dorchester prison, it had one good point – I wouldn't have to go on holiday with Brian and Jane. They had been making me save to pay for my own air-fare to go with them all for a family holiday on the Costa Brava. All I knew, as Jane held out her hand each week, was that it 'Costa Lot'! I was dreading those hours that would be spent on the beach with Jane moaning at everything and Brian trying to keep the peace. I don't think I hated many people, but in the short time I lived with that family I learned to hate them. Such were my feelings toward them that prison was a luxury holiday, compared to the hell they would have made the Costa Brava!

Brian came to see me a few times – I felt, more out of obligation than care. When he came he only moaned at me and told me what a fool I was in missing the 'wonderful holiday'. To be fair, Brian at least made an effort, but Jane had given up on me and, as I had no time for her, I really didn't care.

Dorchester was a typical Victorian prison, complete with its own hanging shed and graveyard! The Youth wing, along with the rest of the prison, was severely over-crowded. Three men occupied cells designed to incarcer-ate one prisoner. Each cell had a bunk bed and a single bed. this meant there was no room to move. In fact the area your bed took up was your personal space. You could spend all day sitting on your bed, as there was lit-erally nowhere else to go. To walk, under escort, down the stairs three times a day to fetch your meals, was the

height of luxury and the full extent of a day's exercise if it
was raining!

There was a toilet block at the end of the wing, consist-
ing of two toilets without any doors for privacy, a urinal
and one shower, again, with no door. There was also a big
sink area with taps that was used to slop out human
waste. The cells, being Victorian, had no toilet facilities,
and during long times of 'bang up' such as night-time,
when only a skeleton team of officers would be on duty,
you would never be allowed out of the cell. This meant
that you had to use the toilet pot that every prisoner is
issued with at induction. To stand and urinate into a pot
in the close confines of a small prison cell and have to do
that in front of two other men is humiliating. However,
it's part of prison life and you have to get used to it
pretty quickly. Every morning, the stench of toilet pots
being emptied of urine was foul. If you were lucky and
were unlocked first, your first priority would be to get to
the wash area before it was reduced to a sewerage works.

Every day was the same, boring lock-up, hour after
hour after hour, with no let-up. Sometimes the boredom
would be violently broken by the shrill sound of the
prison emergency bell. The bell would be sounded if a
fight had broken out and men needed to be separated.
Once the bell sounded, no matter where you were – in the
lunch queue or dripping wet in the shower – every prisoner was quickly locked into their cell until the situation
was dealt with. I had heard about riots in the prison and
was always glad to be locked away when the emergency
bell sounded, as you could not be sure of your personal
safety if you were out of your cell when the bell rang.

Every wing in prison has its drug and tobacco barons.
These are the convicts that spend their time lending tobacco and drugs to other prisoners, but at an astronomical

rate of interest. To ensure they get their interest, they normally 'employ' a couple of heavies to collect the goods owed. The heavies would think nothing of using extreme violence to guarantee the baron receiving what was owed to him. During my prison experience, I would see lots of violence exacted on those foolish enough to borrow, without having the ability to pay back. The prison system was hard and cruel, with many victims falling to 'unexplained' cuts and bruises inside. The weak were picked upon and 'taxed' for protection. When asked if you would like to be protected, if you said no, as you could look after yourself, you could well soon be nursing a bleeding nose! The experienced thugs of the prison regime knew when to strike: normally, just as the screws were doing something else and so would miss any violence.

Some men just couldn't stand the bullying and the fear of being attacked by other prisoners, so they opted for Rule 43. Rule 43 is when a prisoner applies to the Governor to be locked away in segregation from the main prison body for his own protection. Sometimes, if a thug or baron was caught bullying, he would be removed from the wing to protect the rest of the prisoners. Violence was very much a part of the day-to-day life of the prison, and many times I found myself worrying about death threats because I refused to give my tobacco – or 'burn' as it's commonly referred to by the cons – to one of the prison bullies. One man, who shared my cell, was taken into the wash area and shaved literally all over and then punched and kicked. His crime? He confessed to being a homosexual!

> *Violence was very much a part of the day-to-day life of the prison, and many times I found myself worrying about death threats*

The Youth Wing had a six-man cell. This was very unusual in my prison experience, but considered a luxury because there were more windows and more floor space to move around the bunk beds. Once the lights went out at night-time talking was forbidden, but sleep often eluded us, as the bright orange glow of the security lights flooded through the cell windows. I cannot remember one night of darkness during the whole of my time in prison! Although talking was banned, we talked for hours. We planned new crimes, plotted how to rob banks and shared memories of passionate nights with the women in our lives. We would talk into the next day! It would help us escape the harsh reality that liberty had been stripped from us, and give us hope that one day we would be free once again.

One evening we decided that we would hold a séance in our cell, once the lights had gone out. To do this we stole a glass from the wing classroom while we had cleaning duties. We also wrote out all the letters of the alphabet and numbers from zero to nine. In addition to this, we wrote 'yes' and 'no' on two other pieces of paper.

That night, when the lights had been turned off, we leapt from our beds and pulled a cupboard, with a flat Formica top, away from the cell wall. Assembling all the pieces of paper on the flat surface of the cupboard in the form of a Ouija board, I organised the séance. Placing the glass in the middle of the board, I instructed all the men to place one finger each upon the glass. We all began to concentrate quietly, focusing upon the spirit world. Suddenly the glass began to move slowly around the Ouija board. I began to question the spirit and the glass began to spell out the answers. The spirit told us that he had once been a prisoner at Dorchester and that he had committed suicide because he had been very unhappy.

The whole séance was becoming depressive and, as the glass spelled out different answers, I got bored and asked the spirit if he could predict the future. On getting the answer *'Yes'*, I asked the spirit if one of us would die before we reached thirty. It answered *'Yes'*, and so I then asked how that person would die. The glass went to C . . . A . . . N . . . I said cancer and the glass violently sped to 'Yes' on the board. Foolishly, I asked the fateful question: Which one of us would it be? The glass went flying over the surface of the board to one of the men called Stewart and tipped over. The guy nearly died there and then! But before he could, we heard the night screw come onto the landing. We had seconds to get into bed. Hiding the glass in the cupboard and shutting the door, also putting all the pieces of lettered paper in the drawer, we just made it, as the prison officer opened up the security flap and gazed into our cell. Once his footsteps faded into the night we wiped the sweat from our brows, but then something happened that shook us all.

As we heard the clock tower in the centre of Dorchester strike midnight, suddenly the cupboard door flew open with a crash and before our eyes, the glass we had hidden floated out from the back of the cupboard, violently smashing on the floor just where Stewart had been standing! If that wasn't frightening enough, the drawer slid open of its own accord and all the lettered pieces of paper we had used for our Ouija board blew out, slowly floating to the floor like large confetti. One of the men almost wet himself with sheer horror and began to recite the Lord's Prayer.

> *As we heard the clock tower in the centre of Dorchester strike midnight, suddenly the cupboard door flew open with a crash*

The next day, two of the men asked to be transferred to another cell – they were too frightened to stay with us any longer. I knew that the kingdom of darkness was for real, but things that went bump in the night didn't scare me!

Crown Court

The days on remand soon came to an end, and before I knew it, Shane and I were on our way under escort to Bournemouth Crown Court. Once we had been placed in the cellblock deep under the court, drinks were made and we had a brief visit from our solicitors and the defending barristers. We were told that a custodial sentence was very probable, but it would not be too long, due to the fact that we had already been in custody for about four months.

Our names were called and we were led up two flights of steps to a landing just below the dock. At the given signal, we were told to ascend the final steep staircase leading to the infamous dock. The clerk stood and said, 'Court rise'. We all stood as the Judge came in. To our horror it was the same man who had sat at Poole Juvenile court some years before! The charges were duly read, and we had to stand and make our plea. Due to the fact that we were caught red-handed, there was no point in pleading 'not guilty', so we pleaded 'guilty' and were told to sit down again. After what seemed like ages, the Judge retired to consider his sentencing upon us.

When he returned I was asked to stand up. Heart beating wildly, I waited to hear him speak. He began to tell me off, but finally summed up the sentence by ordering me to do 150 hours of 'community service'.

The Judge then told the court that he was being lenient with me due to my troubled family life and the fact that I had already served time as a prisoner remanded in custody. He made it clear, however, that he was noting the sentence, and if I should ever appear before his court again he would have no choice but to give me the maximum sentence! I didn't care about his threat: after all, I would never see him again, or so I thought!

I skipped back down those steep steps to the cells rejoicing at my luck! As I signed for my personal belongings, my solicitor warned me in no uncertain terms that if I didn't conform to the community service order I would be back in court before my feet could touch the ground.

Brian came to fetch me and emphasised how lucky I was and that I should now be very careful who I hung around with, and all the other things I guess parents try to tell their kids at such times.

As we drove home from the court, I was dreading the reunion with Jane. Prison was awful, but living with her was hell! I wouldn't have to put up with her for long though, as I had decided that I would be moving out. Prison had changed me, and now I was going to do my own thing. The social services had had their say for too long: I was now going to make my own way in life. My heart was full of arrogance and pride: although I didn't realise it at the time, the Bible spoke about my condition saying, *'the human heart is most deceitful and desperately wicked'*.[5] That was me, and I was due for a big fall. Yes, the days ahead would take me into the final descent.

7

THE FINAL DESCENT

Liz was about 35 and I was 16, going on 17. She lived up the road from my real mum, and for some reason we just seemed to click. I had popped round one night to mum's house with Colin and as we were drinking tea, a skinny woman came walking in without even knocking and made herself at home. Mum introduced this lady to me as a friend of hers from up the road called Liz. I had been drinking earlier, and before long found myself flirting with this lady, who was almost old enough to be my mother. After Liz had gone I knew I wanted to see her again. my chance came the following week when John, Mum's husband, had some stolen goods to take up to Liz's house and asked me to do it, as he didn't feel well. More likely, he suspected that the police were watching the house and he didn't want to be caught red-handed with a load of 'hot' gear!

Liz came to the door and, by the smell of her breath, she had been on the bourbon, which was her favourite drink. When I entered the front room, I was amazed to see my Uncle Gary lying half drunk on the carpet. It turned out that Uncle Gary had just been released from Dorchester prison and was bringing a message to Liz from her husband Mark, who was doing a stretch for a drug-related crime. Uncle Gary obviously thought his luck was in that night, because he was chatting up Liz as if there were no tomorrow. I felt a challenge rising in me and, although I didn't think this 35-year-old woman would be interested in a 16-year-old boy, I decided to have a go anyway.

Uncle Gary didn't last long, as the drink began to get the better of him, and before long he was sprawled out, snoring on the floor. At this, Liz sat next to me and, within moments, we were kissing, and I found myself in the deep end with a married woman whose husband was in prison. I was excited at the time, as this woman was experienced and knew how to give a young man a good time. I felt neither guilt nor remorse that I was sleeping with another man's wife. I did realise that there would probably be a big fight when her husband was released from prison, but I kept that thought buried deep in my mind, while the power of sexual lust completely took me over. The sad thing is that today, many lose their personal purity through sexual immorality, in a bid to fill the emptiness of their lives. I had plenty of sex, but was I fulfilled? No! happiness eluded me and the deep hunger in my heart for love was never satisfied by my sexual adventures.

One of the things I liked about Liz was that she had 'bottle'. She was fearless in her shoplifting escapades. John had a list of clients who would give their orders to him and then he'd tell Liz what was going to be needed. Liz would 'acquire' the goods and get a percentage of the article's retail value. She had a coat with dummy arms! It sounds crazy, but it worked well for her, as her hands would dart out of her coat and take expensive items, without anybody seeing what had taken place. I was amazed, as she would get hold of a Black and Decker hammer drill and conceal it under her coat in seconds.

Then she would go up to a security guard and ask where the light fittings were!

Before long, I was stealing the 'ordered goods' myself. Shoplifting to order with Liz was both exhilarating and dangerous, as she would often take risks that I wouldn't take. I think that because she had a little daughter, she believed that if she did get caught she wouldn't get a custodial sentence. Every time I walked into a shop with her I knew that I could have been caught. I considered myself to be pretty good, but pride comes before a fall, and I had a big fall coming!

I knew that I was trapped in a lifestyle with which I wasn't happy, but there seemed to be no other way of life open to me. My whole family were crooks, and all I was doing was following in their footsteps.

Drugs and alcohol were part of living. To survive, I needed these 'basics', along with sex and the thrill of crime, and Liz was the same. I had been happy with glue, and then different varieties of cannabis, but although I had every opportunity to buy LSD I never wanted to risk the experience of a 'bad trip'. So, I would get drunk on whisky instead, which for me was safe! Liz, on the other hand, had delved deeper into the misery of drugs, probably through her husband's influence, as he was a dealer. She would go out and buy some 'speed' and then inject herself, using syringes stolen from a local hospital just up the road.

The power of drug addiction is awful and stronger than many can understand. I remember one day when Liz was like a wildcat going crazy for a fix. She was abusive and looking ill, as she was drawn helplessly by the need of the next 'hit'. We drove into Bournemouth looking for the dealers with whom she would normally do business. After an hour of vain searching, Liz was getting desperate. Driving the car dangerously, she swerved up onto the pavement, near the centre of Bournemouth, leapt out of the car and ran after someone walking into the crowd. Moments later, smiling, she jumped back into the car and drove near the sea front. Pulling up outside some men's toilets she jumped out of the car again, this time grabbing me with her. As we stood in the dirty cubical, she mixed the speed in a syringe and pulled down her jeans. In the squalor of that stinking toilet she jabbed the needle into a vein by her crotch. I knew then that I was smarter – this was not the answer to life. I had experienced some drugs, but knew this type of drug taking was not for me.

Driving the car dangerously, she swerved up onto the pavement

The relationship continued – it suited me fine at that young age. I did as I pleased during the day, working and stealing. Then during the evenings, I had as much sex as possible.

The great king of Israel called Solomon had all the money in the world. He had renowned fame and the most beautiful women in the world as his partners in bed. Yet, he was quoted as saying that it was all vanity. He had money, power and sex – the three things that most people are attracted to in the quest for life and satisfaction – yet he was empty. He had climbed to the top, and when he got there he was disillusioned by the view he saw. I, too, was disillusioned with life. I was doing just what I wanted and

He had money, power and sex – the three things that most people are attracted to in the quest for life and satisfaction

yet, through all the drugs, the crime and an active sex life, I was empty and miserable deep within. The hunger and desire for satisfaction needed to be fulfilled, and although I had a full life, in no way was I living life to the full.

Fright Night

My catalogue of crimes worsened by the day and, although I couldn't see it, I was now on a slippery downward spiral. During the day, I would work as a butcher, which I enjoyed, but almost every night I was breaking into a different property. Decency had become a word with which I was no longer familiar, as the crimes became more disgraceful.

One night, on my way to Liz's flat after working at the butcher's, I got a lift from Shane who, although he didn't possess a driving licence, was driving a car borrowed from a homosexual man who was attempting to groom Shane for sexual purposes. We passed by a large undertaker's firm and then I had a brainwave. We would break into this sinister place and see what we could steal. Shane wasn't too sure about it, as he was squeamish, but, being hardened by my experience as a butcher, I was adamant that it was a good idea. I believed that there would be money and also gold and diamond rings, which had been carefully put aside for the relatives of the deceased to collect later. I never once thought about the distress it would cause the grieving families, if they were to be informed that their loved ones' valuables had been stolen whilst in the safekeeping of the undertakers. After having some tea, I mentioned the idea to Liz, who was also squeamish. She said she wanted no part in it. So, after persuading Shane, we both went to the parlour late at night.

The street was busy with people returning home from the pubs, so we could afford the noise of breaking glass as the cars sped by the main road on which the funeral parlour was situated. We jumped over the main wall, ran across the turf and then leapt over the main gates into the complex. Hiding in the shadows, I waited beside a window which had a roller blind pulled down inside. Patiently, I bided my time, clothed in dark jeans and a black leather jacket with matching gloves. I held a hammer in my hand and, just as a large freight lorry from the port rolled past, I smashed the window.

Within seconds, we had climbed through the window, stepping onto broken glass. I penetrated the darkness of that room with the torch I pulled from inside my jacket. There in front of us were three empty slabs. Jackpot! We had got the right room first time. For some, this place would have been creepy, and Shane was beginning to get nervous. I kept reassuring him that dead people couldn't hurt him and that they wouldn't tell any tales either.

Along the side of the room was a long row of cupboards with a top filled with all sorts of surgical instruments of the funeral trade. In the corner was a coffin laid on trestles, lid screwed down and flowers resting on top, that looked creepy, but the best was to come. Along the other wall there were three great doors. I went to the nearest and pulled on the big handle which opened the door and revealed a large fridge. Like most household fridges, a light conveniently came on as the door opened, so I switched off my torch and gazed in.

What a sight! There in front of me were three dead people

What a sight! There in front of me were three dead people. I didn't look for too long, but the mental image of that stayed with me for some time. By now Shane had had enough!

However, I was only just beginning. A sense of macabre boldness had come upon me. I felt that as I had come this far, breaking new barriers of crime by violating the place of the dead, I may as well get as much as I possibly could. I pacified Shane by telling him to look for the keys to the hearse or one of the limousines, explaining we could go for a joyride! While Shane went off in one direction, I went into the hall of the funeral home, and to my surprise, found the office door unlocked.

This was all too easy, and it got better as I slipped into the funeral director's leather swivel chair behind the desk. The desk was locked, but using the claw of the hammer, I had it open very quickly. There was nothing inside the drawer but a leather pouch with a lock on it and it was open! Shining my torch beam onto the pouch in my hand I pulled out about three hundred pounds. Not bad, as I had only been in the place for about ten or fifteen minutes. I tucked the money into the front pocket of my jeans and then went to find Shane. I decided not to tell him about the money. There might be a code among thieves, but I wasn't going to keep it, not tonight anyway! I told Shane that I hadn't found anything and that as the place was giving him the creeps we would leave. Shane readily agreed, as he had no stomach for the break-in anyhow.

That night was another milestone in my callous criminal career. Although I hadn't actually robbed the dead, I had been prepared to do so, and probably would have done if I hadn't struck it rich in the office drawer.

The next day, I was amused to watch the television news, which had reported the burglary in depth, explaining that thieves had received a shock when they broke into the funeral home the night before. They knew this because they had left the fridge door wide open!

House Burglary

Breaking into shops, offices and clubs was one thing, but as my crime spree with Shane escalated, we fixed our sights on people's homes. Shane continued to borrow the Triumph Dolomite from his homosexual friend. I never asked him whether their friendship had become physical, and to be honest I didn't care. As long as we could use the guy's car, it didn't matter. The car was handy, as we found we could go out to more remote homes and, once we established that they were empty, we could strike.

Going through people's drawers and personal effects didn't bother me at all. I had started all those years before at Mr and Mrs Smith's, and progressed from there. Normally we would stick together in one room, searching quickly with our eyes and gloved hands for anything that we might be able to sell or use ourselves. In the week before my last and final arrest, we broke into a few houses every night. I remember in one isolated country house finding a shotgun in the hallway. We sat down in the owner's lounge and enjoyed their Southern Comfort, swigging it straight from the bottle. It was then that I thought of my next plan. We would steal the shotgun and saw off the barrel, and then we could start robbing post offices in the rural areas of Dorset and Hampshire.

The plan was just coming together when we heard the sound of tyres on gravel and saw the headlights of a car through the thin curtains. Like startled rabbits, we dived for the back door, which we had already opened from the inside, and then we were gone, hidden by the darkness of the night. Once we had scrambled into the car, which was parked up the lane, I realised that I had left the gun behind. It was too late, and now it was time to head back to Liz's. That was close, but I'd had many close encounters in my sordid life of deceit and crime, and my escape was not down to luck, but experience, or so I fooled myself.

Undeterred by the night before, Shane and I headed again for the forest area. This time, foolishly, we had drunk a quantity of Scotch and were pretty intoxicated. Thankfully, the roads were empty as we closed in on our next target.

This was a house that Shane had broken into some time before and had been caught! Shane, however, was convinced that there was much jewellery to be had, as the occupier was a rich, single old woman. Standing in the garden, I began to feel nervous. This was not like me, but I sensed that something was wrong. Shane came around the side of the building. He said that he thought the house was empty and that we had better strike now before anyone turned up. With a gloved fist I smashed through a hall window and was in the house within seconds, although a little wobbly because of the drink I had

With a gloved fist I smashed through a hall window and was in the house within seconds, although a little wobbly because of the drink I had consumed. Shane was hot on my tail when it all turned horribly wrong

consumed. Shane was hot on my tail when it all turned horribly wrong.

The door of the lounge opened, and an old lady appeared and began to order us out of her home. I told her not to worry as we were going. She then said she felt ill and we, thinking she might collapse, decided she should lie down and so we helped her to her bedroom. Once we had made her comfortable we knew we had blown it – a house with somebody in! That was never our plan and now we had to escape quickly. Running down the stairs, we ran for the front door and were gone in a flash. The lady, a brave soul, called for help, and so the police were alerted. This was serious, as now the burglary was aggravated by the fact that somebody was at home and had challenged us.

You Can Run But You Can't Hide

It was just a question of time before the police caught up with Shane. The lady had recognised him from a court appearance some time ago. They had picked him up early in the morning and were interviewing him as I was eating my breakfast. It didn't take Sherlock Holmes to work out that serial burglars were operating in that area – and we were in the frame. They also knew, through the woman's testimony, that there were two men involved. Now they were going to work on Shane to find out who the other man was. Although the lady was not hurt in any way and although I had helped her to her room when she felt ill, which was a ploy on her part that worked, it still left the fact that a serious crime had been committed. Given the fact that a string of houses had suffered the same fate, the police threatened Shane with a long custodial sentence. On the other hand, if he co-operated with their inquiries, they would take all that into consideration at his court appearance. It worked, and Shane sang like a little nightingale, giving the police all the information needed to arrest me and give me a tough interrogation. In fact, he basically suggested that I had forced him into the dirty deed, which was rich, considering he planned the hit and actually drove me there, as I couldn't even drive!

I went to work as usual that morning. As a butcher, at a small shop by Poole Quay, I was working on a piece of beef with a boning knife in my hand, when the door opened and in walked two men wearing suits. They asked me if I was Richard Pidgley, and when I replied that I was, they asked me to put my knife down. I did so and they arrested me, reciting the statutory caution. Within moments, two more CID officers came running into the shop from the back entrance. I was handcuffed and bundled into an unmarked police car and driven directly to Poole police station. I was taken to the charging room, frisked thoroughly and made to sign for all my personal effects.

Some CID officers, who had travelled from Ringwood to interview Shane, now wanted to see me, so I was marched into an interview room. The process had begun, and although I had talked and walked from the police before, this time I knew it wasn't going to happen. They knew too many details, and even though I didn't want to think it, I had to accept that Shane had probably grassed me up. After hours of talking, the Forest CID signed for me and under the cover of night drove me to Ringwood police station, where it all started again. I remember looking at the clock on the wall, it was now the early hours and I hadn't admitted anything, but the pressure was beginning to take its toll, as I could hardly keep my eyes open. Finally, I was taken to the cells, which were very old-fashioned and sparse. A thin blanket was all I had to keep me warm through the night.

The next morning as I woke up, my body was craving for a cigarette, but there was no chance of that luxury, not as long as I refused to co-operate with the police. I had a full bladder and needed the toilet. So, feeling miserable, I began to boot the door with my bare feet, as my shoes had been removed. Just when I thought I was going to have to use the cell wall as a urinal, a big uniformed officer entered the small cellblock and began to swear at me for making such a racket so early in the morning. The door opened and he pointed to a dank toilet at the end of the corridor. The officer stood watching me as I used the toilet. I hated that indignity, but I knew I would have to get used to it, because in captivity there is no privacy.

After I had been served breakfast, brought into the station from the bed and breakfast across the road, I was taken into the interview room. The day started with intensive interrogations, and although I kept up my defence, I now realised I was in big trouble and nothing I could do would avert the inevitable.

Shane had told the police just about everything there was to know. By their questioning I knew there was little point in holding out, but I was aware that it was better to be remanded in custody as an unconvicted prisoner, than a convicted one, so I kept quiet and frustrated the police as much as I could.

In the interview room I sat behind a desk, with three officers in the room with me. Once the interview was terminated they went to take me back to my cell. Being rebellious, I defied them, refusing to go. At that they came for me. I had nothing to lose by now, so I kicked over the big wooden table between us and backed into the corner of the room where the breathalysing equipment was stored. I didn't stand a chance against three large Hampshire policemen, but it was worth a go and brought a bit of relief to the boredom of the interview. I punched and kicked, and they gave as good back. Eventually, more policemen bundled into the room, and they carried me back to the cell block, throwing me into my cell with a torrent of verbal abuse.

That night, Shane was brought to the same police station and we talked through the flaps in the cell doors. Although Shane denied grassing me up, I knew it was him. For now it would have to wait, but I determined that vengeance would be mine someday.

That same night, I was marched back into the Ringwood interview room and formally charged with a string of burglaries. Going back to my cell, I thought about all I had done and, with a sigh, I accepted the fact that, 'If you do the crime, you do the time'. Shivering in the cold dark cell, as I drifted into sleep, I welcomed myself to the new world I would be living in for quite some time. A world of locks and keys; a world of absolute captivity; a place where I ceased being a human being with a name but became a prisoner with a number, languishing behind those cold bars, serving out my sentence until every day was paid in full.

If you do the crime, you do the time

Goodbye Liberty – Hello Captivity!

The next day was Saturday, and with much security Shane and I were handcuffed to two large policemen and driven to Ringwood magistrates' court. The room was large and bare, nothing like the grand courtrooms belonging to the Crown at Poole or Bournemouth. The court had about fifteen people inside when we arrived, with three of those sitting behind a table at the front of the room. We sat between the two policemen in front of the magistrates. The clerk read the charges out and we were asked how we pleaded. Both of us pleaded 'Not guilty', which was a joke for Shane as he had confessed everything already to the police at his arrest. The chairman of the magistrates talked quietly to his two colleagues and then told the court that the two prisoners would be remanded in custody at Dorchester prison for a fortnight while reports were being compiled.

As we were led into the foyer of the courthouse, the policemen we were handcuffed to removed the cuffs and then handcuffed Shane and I together. While this was happening, a police transit van or 'meat wagon' as the cons used to call them, was driven onto the forecourt of the court building. This was our chance of escape. I whispered to Shane that we ought to make a run for it and so, as we were led outside into the sunshine, we broke away from the grip of the policemen. Then, all hell broke loose, as the police panicked, fearful of losing two prisoners. The plan was doomed from the beginning, but it was worth having a go. Officers tackled us to the ground and in the struggle I received a bloody nose and scratched face. The doors of the police van were flung open and we were literally thrown head first into the back of the van. One of the officers who climbed in with us tightened the handcuffs to the extent that the blood supply almost stopped flowing into our hands. As the cuffs dug deep into our wrists we were told to 'Behave or else'. When we agreed to sit properly and not try any more tricks, the handcuffs were finally loosened.

Then, all hell broke loose, as the police panicked

Looking out of the window, I gazed at the beautiful Dorset countryside on my way to Dorchester prison. Up until now I had never appreciated it, because my seedy

world of sin and crime had blinded me to the beauty star-
ing at me in the face all the time. Stripped of everything,
including my very liberty, I began to long for the freedom
of just walking down a country lane and listening to the
birds singing: a pleasure that costs nothing but would
now elude me for literally years.

As we rolled up to the great gates of Dorchester prison,
situated in Barrack square, just a stone's throw from the
centre of Dorchester itself, I felt a sense of despair flood
my thoughts. I was entering another world. People walking about in the street outside would forget me. Who cares
about prisoners? I could die in there and it wouldn't
matter to anybody at all.

By now I was like an 'old lag' at the age of seventeen. I
hated induction, but knew the ropes all too well: standing
naked in front of the screws and the indignity of the officers checking every part of your anatomy for concealed
drugs; the paperwork that took forever; the bath; the
rough towels; the prison uniform that was always too
large and shoes that never fitted properly; waiting in a
holding cell with nothing to do until a prison officer took
you into the main prison block. Yes, I hated induction, but
I would have to accept whatever came to me in this world
of locks and bars.

After being processed through induction I was taken to
a cell with Shane. This time, because of space problems in
the Youth Wing, we were placed on the ground floor by
the main food-serving area. This turned out to be a good
location, as we got our meals first, and as the older convicts serving up the prison food called us 'Baby Burglars',
we normally got a good portion of piping hot food.

The next morning, after breakfast, I was escorted to the
Principal Officer's office. Once inside and the door shut,
the officer went through all the details of my case and

then told me my prison number, J52327. From then on, I was a number and no longer a person. The luxury of a first name is unheard of in prison; every time I had to report to a prison officer I had to say 'J52327 Pidgley, Sir.'

My name was all I had left. Everything else had been taken from me, and so the final act of dehumanising me had taken

> *The officer went through all the details of my case and then told me my prison number, J52327. From then on, I was a number and no longer a person*

place. I would no longer be called Richard until months later, when I began to have a regular prison visitor come to see me at Aylesbury.

After that first fortnight at Dorchester, we were driven back to Ringwood Magistrates Court for another hearing. This was a waste of time for us, because we had to go through the procedure of paperwork and being processed for the court appearance. It was a waste of time, because the court promptly sent us back to prison on remand for yet another fortnight, while reports were still being compiled. At least we got out of our cell and had a day's ride through the New Forest! No wonder the taxpayer gets so irate at the wastage of the nation's financial resources when it's funding prisoners' day trips.

I'd had the inner strength to get through my time in prison before, but this time things all got too much for me. For a start, I had no idea how long I would have to wait until my court appearance which, because of my previous criminal record, was now certainly going to be at Bournemouth Crown Court. And secondly, I was angry with Shane for grassing me up to the police. He was still denying it, but I knew he had done it, and the smouldering fire of revenge in my heart was being fanned by the wind of anger, day by day. In the end I got to the stage where I felt I could not eat, such was the anger inside me towards Shane. For a fortnight, I collected my food and then threw it out of the window for the birds, because my appetite was gone. It was replaced by awful visions of violent vengeance on Shane.

I had this daily waking dream of following Shane into a room, away from other people, and then plunging a butcher's boning knife into his abdomen, slicing through his liver and kidneys. I could feel his hot blood on my hands as it spurted and pumped out all over my clothes. The daily vision of murdering Shane gave me hope; hope that I would one day be released to exact such a terrible revenge upon the man I had once considered a friend. I made my secret plans to get Shane, and meditated upon them daily, considering where and when I would strike and then how I would fix an alibi and use a fire to burn all my bloodstained clothes.

> *Plunging a butcher's boning knife into his abdomen, slicing through his liver and kidneys. I could feel his hot blood on my hands as it spurted and pumped out all over my clothes*

Day by day the vision became clearer, and nearly became a reality as, one day, after dinner, Shane and I fell out and I exploded angrily and violently.

Shane had said something and that had set me off. Within a split second I had leapt from my bunk to his in our small cell and was grappling with him. My hands now around his throat, I began to squeeze the very life breath out of him. As he frantically fought for air, he got lucky as his right hand smashed into the emergency bell on the cell wall by the door. I continued to fight with

Shane as we crashed to the floor, still with my hands fixed firmly around his throat. It was a small miracle for me that the door opened, and prison officers rushed in, dragging me off Shane. If they had not intervened, I could well have been in prison to this very day serving a life sentence for murder!

It was obvious that I was the one who had started the fight, and so I was roughly marched to a dungeon cell in the prison. The punishment block, or dungeon as we called it, was built at a lower level than the other ground-floor cells. In fact, the window was very high up in the cell wall, with bars that were almost on the outside ground level. This made the room very dark and oppressive, and led to despair in any captive inside. I was flung in with a torrent of threats from the screws as they slammed the door shut on me.

As I sank to the floor, I felt absolutely alone and totally isolated, knowing that I could be in there for days, languishing in those dark, dank and depressive surrounds. Up to this point, I had been the big mouth, the rebel, but now I felt rotten and so empty inside. My life flashed before my eyes: everything came back to me in my mind like a slide show, and I felt that my whole life was a waste of space. I was empty, I was ruined, and I had nothing in the world. talk about poor: I didn't even have a name, just a prison number. I didn't know how long I was going to be in the dungeon, and I honestly felt that I could no longer cope with life. Nobody loved me or cared about me, and as far as the screws were concerned I was worthless scum.

Such darkness flooded my soul then, that suicide seemed the only way out. There was a real presence of evil and darkness in that cell; an evil that seemed to put me under a spell. The devil had no more use for me now, so his last action would be to destroy me. Enough was enough. A sickening sense of lostness and failure flooded my already dark, cold and empty heart. In a moment I had lost the will to live. As I reflected on seventeen years, I realised that I was a waster, a nobody going nowhere, and I wanted out.

As if in a trance I ripped the sheet off the bed. I rolled the sheet up into a makeshift rope, tying one end in a slip-knot and then binding the other end to the bars in the small window high up on the cell wall. I stood on the radiator pipe with the rope around my neck and I tottered forward into a certain and most painful death of suffoca-tion. And then it happened! I can't fully explain it, but it seemed as if a strong, powerful and yet invisible hand pushed me back against the cell wall. The hand, if it was a hand, then lifted the rope from my neck and let me slide gently to the floor. I don't know how much later it was, but finally the door opened and prison officers rushed in. On seeing the rope still attached to the prison bars, they stripped me naked and forced some medicine down my throat. Then they put me into a padded cell, still naked, with a sort of quilted blanket as my only source of covering and warmth. Later, I realised that God had saved me from suicide and a certain hell.

> *I stood on the radiator pipe with the rope around my neck and I tottered forward*

The Power of Prayer

Much later, I was amazed to hear that my strange experi-ence in the Dorchester dungeon was an extraordinary answer to prayer. Somebody at a large Baptist church in

Bournemouth had read about my case in the local paper. Reading the details of my disturbing case history, they realised my life was broken and empty. Then, with a real concern for me, because I was in so much trouble, they told the other members of the church about my situation and they all started praying for me.

God heard the faithful prayers of those people who cared about me, even though they didn't know me. They had actually been praying for me at the time I was in the dungeon cell! Little did they know that God would not only save me from suicide, but also save me from my sins and call me to the ministry. That's why the Bible also encourages us to pray by saying, *'Now glory be to God! By his mighty power at work within us, he is able to accomplish infinitely more than we would ever dare to ask or hope.'*[6]

After the suicide attempt, I was escorted to Winchester prison. The prison was known for its very large hospital wing, which caged some strange prisoners indeed, including me!

Once I was processed at Winchester, I was taken to my cell, which was actually quite pleasant. Well, pleasant after the dungeon and padded cell I had found myself in just days before. An officer and two inmates brought meals to my cell. Talk about room service! Yet all was not good, as that place was full of darkness and depression. As I got to slop out my chamber pot that night just before lights out, I saw, briefly, a young man in the cell adjoining mine. Early the next morning there was a lot of

The young man who I had seen hours before was being cut down and his corpse removed from the cell

confusion outside my neighbouring cell. The young man who I had seen hours before was being cut down and his corpse removed from the cell. That hospital wing was reserved for the crazy and suicidal and I was in the midst of it all. Although the cell was nice, light and warm, the atmosphere was awful, with a depressive heaviness that seemed to soak into everything.

After a week, one morning I was told that I was going to the 'Doll's House', which was the nickname for the Youth Wing of Winchester prison. Settling into my new cell, I soon made friends with the other young man who would be sharing the same air and space for the foreseeable future. The days went quickly in the Doll's House. I was given the job of cleaning the 'M1', which was the main corridor that ran along the whole length of the Youth wing block. The job got me out of my cell for most of the morning, which was a welcome break from the confines of a small two-man cell. The floor had to be swept, mopped and then polished to a sparkling shine so that you could almost see your face in it.

My barrister came to see me at Winchester. He told me very plainly that I didn't stand a chance pleading 'Not guilty'. It would be better for me if I took it like a man and owned up to what he knew I had done. I realised that he was right and so agreed to his counsel. He warned me that I would probably get a long sentence because of the way I had openly broken the community service imposed upon me at my last appearance at Bournemouth Crown Court. I knew that I was in for the high jump this time, and so mentally prepared myself for the worst, which could be years inside prison.

The Sentence

By now, Shane had also been brought to the Doll's House, and the day of our court appearance came. We were handcuffed together and escorted under guard from Winchester prison to Bournemouth Crown Court in a transit van. The van went straight to the prisoners' entrance, which was below ground level. In the underground cells, we waited for our case to be called. By now I was feeling nervous, and a cold sweat broke out all over my body. Shivering in my cell I finally heard footsteps coming towards me. Both Shane and I were warned about attempting to escape and how futile it would be. Then we climbed two flights of narrow stairs onto a landing. There was a small flight of steps still to climb, which led directly into the dock. We were like actors in the wings of a theatre waiting for our cue. The signal was given and we climbed the last steps into the dock and surveyed the half-full courtroom.

The clerk said, 'Court rise', and we all stood as three robed and wigged men walked from a side door into the courtroom and took their place at the bench. Our names were read out, and we had to answer to them. Then, all the charges were read out. They seemed to go on and on, and the newspaper reporter probably had a job to scribble it all down. Once the charges were read out, we then had to let it be known to the court how we were going to plead, 'Guilty' or 'Not guilty'. As I stood before the judges, I was horrified to see that the one sitting to the right was the same judge who had sentenced me to community service only months earlier. He had warned me that if I ever came into his court again he would give me the maximum sentence. I knew that it was hopeless to try to talk my way out of the situation and impossible to escape, as there were two prison officers in the dock and policemen at the court door. Resigning myself to whatever would happen next, I pleaded 'Guilty'. I sat down, and the next few hours all seemed to be a blur.

Finally, after much reviewing of all I had done, I was asked if I had anything to say. I rose to my feet and began to apologise for everything I had done; saying sorry to all the people I had committed crimes against. The judges then retired to consider the sentencing, and I was taken back down to my cell in the basement of the building.

I was no longer feeling afraid at this point. After all, there was absolutely nothing I could do to alter things, and the clock could never be turned back. So I waited in my cell. One of the screws – a friendly one – came along and joked that I only had to worry if the judge came back in with a black cap on! He gave me a cigarette, and as I smoked it, suddenly we were called back up to the court. The clerk said his customary 'Court rise' and we all stood to our feet again. When the judges had taken their place at the bench everyone was asked to sit.

Then the judge seated in the middle asked me to stand and he proceeded to formally sentence me. I can't remember all he said, but the words 'four years' kept ringing in my head. Four years, can you imagine being sentenced to four years in prison? Whether you deserve it or not, four years is still a long stretch for a young person to come to terms with. The only thing that softened that mighty blow was that when Shane was asked to stand, he, too, was sentenced to four years' imprisonment.

I finally felt that justice, in a strange sort of way, had been done. The man who had grassed me up to the police, thinking he would get off with a lighter sentence, was given the same as me! The joy of knowing that he, too, would have to do his 'bird' (prison slang for time in jail), brought immense comfort to me as I skipped down the steps, returning to my basement cell. That night, after tea in the prison cells at Bournemouth Crown Court, we were escorted under guard once again to Dorchester prison. The induction process over, we were taken to the same cell that we had been in weeks before. So much had happened that day that I really didn't have the energy to worry about the implications of such a long sentence. I put my head upon my pillow and fell asleep.

The next day I was marched into the Principal Officer's office, and he went through the details of my sentencing, explaining that if I behaved myself in prison I could be out after maybe two and a half years. I was also told that because I was now doing a long prison stretch, Dorchester prison could no longer house me, and so I was being transferred the next day to Aylesbury Youth Custody Centre, where I would serve the rest of my sentence.

8

THE GREATEST DISCOVERY

The long drive from Dorchester prison to Aylesbury youth custody centre was a joy. Beautiful fields and trees flanked the roadsides and, as the prison van sped on its way, cutting through the countryside, I drank in all I could see, marvelling at the vast open spaces after the confines of Dorchester's exercise yard.

I had never been into the county of Buckinghamshire before, and now here I was being driven under escort, all courtesy of Her Majesty the Queen! The four screws were in a good mood: the escort duty broke up the daily monotony of herding prisoners in and out of different cellblocks. They actually gave us a few cigarettes to smoke on the journey, which was normally unheard of in the prison.

I had a feeling that all was going to be well at Aylesbury Youth Custody centre, unlike the despairing feeling of Dorchester prison. I didn't know it then, but I was about to make the greatest discovery of my lifetime – a discovery so great that it would change my life forever!

As the prison van drove into Aylesbury, approaching the prison gates along the main road, I tried to retain a mental picture of the outside of the prison. I looked long and hard at those impregnable walls topped with razor wire, and those great wooden and iron gates, making the place a fortress to the outside world and keeping me inside as a prisoner for what might well be a period of three years. The driver sounded the horn and a small door opened in the left-hand door of the great gates. A prison officer emerged and took the details from our driver. Moments later, the gates opened and in we drove. That was the last time I would see the real world for years.

> *I looked long and hard at those impregnable walls topped with razor wire*

The gatehouse consisted of two great gates, with enough space in between for a minibus to park. They were never opened at the same time in case some prisoner felt the temptation to break the 100 metres sprint record! However, a year on from that day I did get to see both gates opened at once.

It happened one day while I was cleaning the chief officers' corridor as a trusted prisoner. The fire alarm had gone off and two fire engines came, as was procedure, alerted by the sirens. I gazed through the open door of the main office block and, for a moment, saw the outside world, as the engines screamed through the gatehouse.

Induction

Induction at Aylesbury was no different to that at any other prison in which I had been. Standing in front of the induction officers, I had to strip off all my clothes and go through the same humiliation as before. The bathhouse was pleasant though. It was through a door into a different room, and because there were only Shane and me to be 'processed', there was no rush to be 'sheep-dipped'. I sank into the warm water of the bath and enjoyed those moments immensely, away from the ever-watchful eyes of prison officers. You get only one bath when you go to prison, and that's when you get processed in the induction wing. After that, it's a shower once a week for a maximum of five minutes, if you're lucky.

I could have soaked for hours, but it wasn't to be, as the induction officer told us to hurry up. Once dried off – and this time with the modesty of a towel wrapped around my middle – I was led to a third room filled with shelves of prison clothing. I was asked my size, and amazingly, they actually found clothes that fitted me. Second-hand, of course, but at least they fitted! White underpants, woollen socks, a faded blue tee shirt, blue denim jeans with a matching denim jacket and a pair of black shoes. I was also kitted out with a plastic knife, fork and spoon set, a plastic mug, a towel, a comb and a pair of pyjamas. Armed with all my new things, I was ordered to follow the officer onto the upstairs landing of the induction wing.

There were ten cells along that landing, each designed to house one prisoner while they served their two weeks of induction training at Aylesbury prison. My cell was spartan, with one bed, a small cupboard unit with a drawer, cupboard and towel rail, a plastic jug, washbowl and toilet pot – thankfully fitted with a lid. I was told to make myself at home, for presently someone would be along to see me. In fact, over the next few days, I saw quite a few different people associated with the prison. The assistant governor came along, one of the principal officers, a psychoanalyst (probably to confirm I was crazy!), the chaplain, the doctor and the wing officer. The wing officer was quite strict, and as he went through all the rules for me, he told me that nobody had escaped from the prison, and if he caught me trying to, he would personally break my arms and legs! After our 'friendly' chat, I decided there and then I wouldn't ever try to escape.

Induction is hated by most of the cons (prisoners) because it means you are locked up for long periods of time with nothing to relieve the boredom. In fact, you only get to leave your cell for the three daily meal times. Even then you only have to go down a flight of stairs into the main prison area and collect your food from a serving bay. Once you had eaten your food it was back to your cell again for more 'bang up', as we called it. If the weather was good, we were able to go into the bottom exercise yard for a walk, but that was only for half an hour. Because of bad weather, we were only able to go out there about three times in the fortnight I was held on the induction wing. Induction was also hated because you were deprived of the right to work, so you couldn't earn any money, and without money you are helpless if you want to buy cigarettes, which is what almost every con craves.

The prison authority didn't want a riot on their hands though, so they graciously gave every prisoner on induction about £1.03 per week. With that, you had just enough money to buy half an ounce of Old Holborn rolling tobacco, a packet of Rizlas (cigarette papers) and a box of safety matches. In the interest of security the swan vesta type were banned, due to their explosive nature. The problem was that you had to roll the cigarettes very thin to make the 'burn' (prison slang for tobacco) last you the whole week – which took great discipline. Also, the matches always ran out. To overcome that problem every con learns the art of match-splitting. Taking a razor, you carefully splice the match into two and then, for the experienced lag – as I had become – you do it a second time. A box of 40 matches now becomes a box of 160. Sometimes the head of the match would fall off the splinter to which it was attached, and that would make things very tricky. You can't stick it back on, not in prison anyway. It happened to me on many occasions, often when it was late at night and it was the only match I had left. Now that's a disaster!

Craving for nicotine and having a broken match means one thing – satisfaction only comes through pain. With a sweaty fingertip pressed into the broken incendiary of the match head and the cigarette in your mouth, you use your finger as the match. You have a split second to ignite the cigarette and draw on the smoke as the match literally lights up on the end of your finger, burning the flesh in sharp pain. Such was my deep dependence on nicotine, I would often resort to such emergency tactics to have a smoke. Often, through prison days when I had run out of 'burn', I would walk along the corridors with my eyes to the ground like an eagle. If I saw the butt end of a stamped out cigarette, I would swoop down to pick it up, grovelling and humiliating myself as I would later smoke the butt end to feed my powerful habit.

Thinking back, I remembered saying that I could quit smoking at any time. Yet, at that time I was reduced to such levels of depravity to satisfy the hunger and need for nicotine. Young people are seduced by the cool and sexy look of blue smoke exhaled by the smoker, unaware of the vice-like grip it places upon its unsuspecting victim. Yes, induction was a killer, but if you could mentally endure its painful boredom you stood a chance of doing your bird.

After all the interviews had taken place, I resigned myself to the incredible boredom that was now to come. Sitting on my bunk, I looked around my new cell. There were a few items that had already caught my eye: the cupboard in which to put my towel and spare underwear, a plastic water jug and mug, a washbowl and a toilet pot – nothing else. No cigarettes, no magazines, in fact, nothing at all. Then I spotted a red book that was lying on the floor by the cupboard. I wasn't in the mood for reading, but anything was better than the desperate craving for nicotine, or going insane with boredom. I looked at the book, and to my disgust saw that it was a Gideon Bible! Without thinking, I stretched from my bunk and took the Bible from the floor.

I looked at the book, and to my disgust saw that it was a Gideon Bible!

Something strange happened as I picked up the Gideon Bible: I actually had this inexplicable desire to read it. This was alien to me, as I had never desired to read the Bible before. I had stolen a Bible once, from Operation Mobilisation's boat *Logos* as she was berthed at Poole Quay, when I was at the children's home, but when I couldn't sell it to anyone I simply heaved it into a skip by the side of the road.

I began to read the Bible, starting in one of the Gospels purely by chance and not by choice, as this was where the bible had opened when I picked it up. I read about the man called Jesus Christ, who was doing amazing things. He actually healed people: the blind received their sight and the lame leapt for joy as Jesus' power made them well. Amazing as it seemed, I read about Jesus doing the impossible like raising the dead. In fact, those Bible pages were full of and focused on all the incredible miracles that Jesus performed. Best of all, Jesus was seen to be making time for people who were considered outcasts by everyone else. Could I be reading right?

I didn't need to be a theologian to understand that God wasn't happy with my behaviour. In fact, God's son, Jesus Christ, went to great lengths to teach righteous living and was quick to condemn sin! As my eyes soaked up those golden words, I grasped this wonderful truth: God loved me and he wanted me to give up my wretched, poor lifestyle so that I could receive his forgiveness. This was amazing! The words that I read and re-read burned in my heart: in fact, I couldn't put the Bible down. I'd had powerful experiences of the dark occult world. I knew the intoxicating power of liquor and the rush and euphoria that drugs had brought into my life, but this Bible was something else! I had never touched anything like this before: the Bible seemed to be a living book and I was compelled to keep reading page after page after page.

Revelation

As I read the Bible, the verses came alive to me. One such verse that deeply touched my heart was from the Gospel of John, when Jesus spoke about the love of God to a religious man hungry for spiritual truth. *'For God so loved the world that he gave his only Son, so that everyone who believes in him will not perish but have eternal life.'*[7]

Revelation dawned upon the darkness of my soul. Yes, God loved me! I couldn't get that amazing fact out of my mind. Yes, God Almighty, the Creator of Heaven and Earth, actually loved a lowlife such as me!

I later understood the wonderful words of the hymn writer, C. H. Gabriel, who wrote

I stand amazed in the presence of Jesus the Nazarene,
And wonder how he could love me, A sinner, condemned, unclean.
Oh how marvellous! Oh how wonderful! And my song shall
    ever be;
Oh how marvellous! Oh how wonderful! Is my Saviour's love
    for me!

As I read about the earthly ministry of Jesus Christ among ordinary people I was amazed. Now, however, the Gospel account began to rise to a dramatic climax as Jesus was arrested, tried and cruelly crucified on a wooden cross. At his arrest Jesus said that he could have called on thousands of angels to rescue him, but he didn't. Jesus knew only too well that his death on the cross was all part of God's plan to bring man back to himself from the dark paths of sin. The Bible explained that Jesus' death on the cross was all about God loving me, and proving that love, by taking the punishment I rightly deserved for all the wrong I had ever done.

The cross of Jesus Christ made a deep impact on my life. Love, so I am told, can be measured by what someone is prepared to give, or give up, for another person. The television commercial cashes in on this with the now famous advert for the Nestlé chocolate company's product 'Rolos': with the two little sweethearts and the final catch phrase, 'Do you love anyone enough to give them your last Rolo?' Well God did love us,

The cross of Jesus Christ made a deep impact on my life

enough to give us his only son to die in our place. This was love not merely in words, which we all know can mean very little, but a powerful demonstration of God's love that would change the history of the world.

Years later, a preacher illustrated this wonderful truth by telling a story about a bridge-keeper in Germany who had the responsibility of operating a large rail swing bridge over a river. The keeper, on being alerted of a train approaching, would use great gear wheels kept in a pit to move the massive bridge into the right position spanning the river, thus allowing a train to pass over the water safely. The keeper would salute the passing train with all its city passengers on their way home from work and they would wave back to him.

One day during the school holidays, his son, a young boy, went to watch his dad at work. Being alerted to a train speeding towards the bridge, the dad went, as usual, to operate the machinery that moved the bridge into position. Almost immediately, he heard a pitiful scream as he pulled a gear lever. It had come from the pit containing the massive gear wheels. Running to the pit, he looked down and to his sickening horror saw his young son helplessly entangled in the mechanism.

The keeper knew that it would take many men, and probably hours, to free the trapped boy and there was no time. Unless he moved the bridge, the train would go crashing into the river, causing great loss of life; if he did move the bridge it would kill his son. The agonising decision was made instantly. With a pain that threatened to rip out his own heart, the bridge-keeper moved the bridge and crushed the life out of his beloved small son. With seconds to spare, the bridge was positioned as the train came rumbling down the track. The whistle blew, the engine driver and fireman waved and the people waved as usual to the keeper. They couldn't see the hot tears streaming down his face soaking his beard. 'Don't they know about my son?' thought the keeper as the train sped away to its destination.

There came a day in heaven when God, the divine 'bridge-keeper', seeing the 'train' full of fallen mankind fast approaching the 'river of judgement and death', leapt into action and allowed his son to die sacrificially in our place. We should have paid for our own sins by dying the death God's holiness and righteousness requires. Yet God paid for us all.

The Bible records God's unchanging character as love. The Apostle John wrote to the first Christians telling them 'God is love'. Jesus, himself, as he approached Jerusalem, the city of his execution, knowing the full horror of what awaited him at the cross, said to his disciples, *'Greater love hath no man than this, that a man lay down his life for his friends.'* [8]

I didn't have to be a Bible college student to understand that God not only deeply loved me, but also wanted me to turn from my sinful lifestyle in sincere repentance. God wanted me to enjoy a whole new life through his son, Jesus Christ, who was the only way to eternal life. As the days went by, I kept reading the Bible. Things that used to intimidate me, such as my cramped cell with its oppressive bars, and the prison officers, no longer bothered me at all. As I was now totally absorbed by the Gideon Bible I had found in my cell.

Induction passed quickly and before I knew it I was transferred to the second landing of A wing known as A2. As I bundled my things together and followed the senior officer into the main prison block, the Gideon Bible came with me. I had found true treasure in the Bible, and I wasn't going to let go of it at any cost.

Salvation Immense and Free

One night, 19th December 1984, as I was reading the Bible before the lights went out, the words from the Apostle John's first letter hit me straight between the eyes:

> *This is the message he has given us to announce to you: God is light and there is no darkness in him at all. So we are lying if we say we have fellowship with God but go on living in spiritual darkness. We are not living in the truth. But if we are living in the light of God's presence, just as Christ is, then we have fellowship with each other, and the blood of Jesus, his Son, cleanses us from every sin. If we say we have no sin, we are only fooling ourselves and refusing to accept the truth. But if we confess our sins to him, he is faithful and just to forgive us and to cleanse us from every wrong.*[9]

That was it, I knew I had to get right with God and ask Christ into my heart to be my Saviour. Up until that point, nobody had ever preached to me, nor had anyone ever counselled me, but the Word of God, which is living and active, worked deep down in my life. Each word was like a beam of light bringing life and light into the darkness of my sinful being. Behind the high walls of this prison in Aylesbury, I had encountered the Living God in my small prison cell through his eternal Word, the Bible. That night I got on my knees, on the cold hard floor and began to cry out to God. I didn't really know how to pray, but then as one modern Bible translation puts it, '*And when you come before God, don't turn that*

> *That was it, I knew I had to get right with God and ask Christ into my heart to be my Saviour*

into a theatrical production either. All these people making a regular show out of their prayers, hoping for stardom! Do you think God sits in a box seat? Here's what you should do: find a quiet, secluded place so you won't be tempted to role-play before God. Just be there as simply and honestly as you can manage. The focus will shift from you to God, and you will begin to sense his grace.[10]

That's how everyone should pray – being totally honest with the God who created you, focussing on his love for you and his willingness to listen to all those who call on his name in sincerity, believing he will hear and answer prayer. And so I, for the first time ever in my life cried out to God. I held nothing back as I confessed all my filthy, rotten sins that had separated me from God; sins that had robbed me of life for more than eighteen years.

My sins had caused much suffering to the one who was perfect and absolutely holy. There is no love like the love of God, and I knew that the emptiness and pain of all my years was now over. For at the cross of Jesus Christ there was hope. Tears began to flow down my cheeks as I realised what a mess my life was in before God's holy and awesome presence. Yes, the tears flowed freely as I grasped the reality of Jesus' awful pain and death upon the cross, which was endured for sinners such as me to buy my freedom from emptiness and death.

Salvation is not something we achieve, but rather something we receive

The truth is, salvation is not something we achieve, but rather something we receive. So at the foot of the cross, looking by faith to Jesus Christ, I received the forgiveness of God and a whole new life. God heard my cry of repentance and faith, as he promises to hear any who call to him.

Those were precious moments indeed for me in my prison cell, for as I basked in the light of God's grace and mercy, angel choirs sang the praises of a saving God in heaven. It was then, at that moment, Jesus Christ, the Son of God did two wonderful things for me.

Firstly, he wrote my name in his 'Book of Life'.[11] My name had been recorded at New Scotland Yard, along with my fingerprints, and probably still is, as a felon. However, in heaven there is a book, the greatest book in the universe, called 'The Book of Life', and my name was recorded in that book the instant I repented and believed in Jesus Christ as my Saviour. If you are ever granted the privilege of turning the pages of that celestial book, turn to 19th December 1984. Cast your eye down the page and you will see my name, 'Richard Pidgley', and by the side of it written the wonderful word that summed up my experience, 'Forgiven'.

Secondly, not only did the Son of God write my name in his 'Book of Life', but he also came into my heart. For too long, God was at a distance, but now he was with me and in me. Jesus said, *'Look! Here I stand at the door and knock. If you hear me calling and open the door, I will come in, and we will share a meal as friends.'*[12]

The world-famous painter, Holman Hunt, captured that scripture with his great renowned painting, 'The Light of the world' where Jesus is portrayed standing outside an old, weed overgrown door, holding a lamp in his hand. There is no handle on the outside, signifying that if Christ is to gain entry, it can only be initiated by us opening the door from the inside. Although God is sovereign and all-powerful and he can do anything he wants, he created us with free will so that we can make up our own minds about him. God doesn't force himself upon people but he knocks on the door of every heart: sometimes through the Bible, other times through preaching in churches, or a radio or television programme. Some people hear God knocking when friends testify about God's grace and their Saviour Jesus Christ.

For years I failed to hear the knocking of a persistent Saviour, but now, I am sure glad that the day came when I heard him loud and clear and threw open the door of my heart allowing him free access to all that I am.

Instantly, I knew that I was saved! This was not mere emotion, although I was very emotional and tearful, but rather a faith focussed on the work Jesus Christ accomplished by dying on the cross for my sins and rising from the dead on the third day for my justification.

People aren't saved through emotions, but by faith. That's why the Bible clearly says, *'For if you confess with your mouth that Jesus is Lord and believe in your heart that God raised him from the dead, you will be saved. For it is by believing in your heart that you are made right with God, and it is by confessing with your mouth that you are saved.'*[13]

I knew that I had been totally forgiven. Every sin I had committed was washed away through the blood of Jesus Christ. Some of the things I did were so heinous I couldn't even write about them in this book. Things that would have condemned me to a lost eternity, sins that shouted loudly in my face 'Guilty' and would have made me endure the everlasting fire of hell. For hell is the abode of the damned, the place of everlasting conscious punishment in the fiery lake of burning sulphur.

Preachers have been accused of painting wrong pictures of hell and its fires of eternal torments. But they are only following the example of Christ, who graphically painted word pictures of hell to warn people of what would certainly come to all sinners who rejected the mercy of God. It never ceases to amaze me how people see the wrong in others and fail to see their own weaknesses. 'I'm a good sinner,' some have told me, fully believing that somehow they will escape the coming judgement.

There are two places for the dead to go – either heaven or hell. Heaven is a prepared place for prepared people. Forgiven sinners enter into the joy of heaven through the grace of God, brought to man by Jesus Christ's sacrificial death. Unforgiven sinners, who despise Jesus' mercy and offer of life, end up in hell, forever separated from God and in eternal torment.

The greatest words Jesus ever said to anyone were, 'My son, your sins are forgiven.'[14] That's the incredible thing – a lifetime of wrongdoing can be put right in a moment. Some people find it hard to accept that God will give them a pardon from every sin they have ever committed. Once we receive Jesus Christ as our Saviour, God no longer deals with us as our sins deserve, but he forgives us freely and fully. In fact, King David, who had become an adulterer and murderer, after making confession to God, spoke about God's forgiveness in the Psalms: *'The Lord is merciful and gracious; he is slow to get angry and full of unfailing love. He will not constantly accuse us, or remain angry forever. He has not punished us for all our sins, nor does he deal with us as we deserve. For his unfailing love toward those who fear him is as great as the height of the heavens above the earth. He has removed our rebellious acts as far away from us as the east is from the west.'*[15]

There was so much I had done wrong. Hundreds of people had been hurt by my callous crimes. Thousands of pounds worth of damage had been done to property; all those broken windows and jemmied doors that needed to be replaced. Broken-hearted people surveying their homes in the wake of my trail of burglary had felt violated and insecure in their own homes. Was it possible that I could be forgiven? God can forgive some, but what about people such as me, who are regarded as the scum of society. I was the sort of person they wanted to lock up and throw away the key. Could I be forgiven? Yes, with God there is forgiveness.

Later on, as I counselled a young man in the prison with another Christian inmate, he broke down, telling us that he had murdered his mum and could never be forgiven. What joy came to his face as we told him the greatest news ever: the blood of God's son, Jesus Christ, has power to cleanse us from all sin. In fact, there is no sin that, when repented of, cannot be dealt with by the blood of Jesus Christ.

Maybe, as you are reading this book right now, you are holding onto a dark secret, a burden, a sin committed and never confessed, and the weight of guilt is crushing your soul, robbing you of peace. Some sins are so depraved you would never think of speaking to a minister about them, lest he recoils from you in sheer horror. Yet, with God, there is mercy. His grace allows you the chance of repentance and the opportunity for you to come clean with him about your sins. Whatever you have done, know this – there is forgiveness with God; you can be made clean through the blood of Jesus. The world has many religions on offer for the spiritually hungry, but none of them offers hope for the guilty sinner awaiting judgement and hell fire, nor the peace and joy that comes with God's forgiveness.

At a great parliament of religions held in Chicago many years ago, practically every known religion was represented. During one session, Dr Joseph Cook of Boston, suddenly arose and said: 'Gentlemen, I beg to introduce to you a woman with a great sorrow.

Bloodstains are on her hands and nothing she has tried
will remove them. The blood is that of murder. She has
been driven to desperation in her distress. Is there
anything in your religion that will remove her sin and
give her peace?' A hush fell upon the gathering. Not one
of the company replied. Raising his eyes heavenwards,
Dr Cook then cried out, 'John, can you tell this woman
how to get rid of her awful sin?' The great preacher waited, as if listening for a reply. Suddenly he cried, 'Listen,
John speaks, "The blood of Jesus Christ, his Son, cleanses
us from all sins."' Not a soul broke the silence: the repre-
sentatives of Eastern religions and Western cults sat
dumb. In the face of human need, the Gospel of Jesus
Christ alone could meet the need. The sin of the race
demanded the blood of Christ.

From that moment in my cell on 19th December 1984, I
knew a peace and a joy that I hadn't dreamed existed.
Psalm 32 starts with, 'O what joy for those who are forgiven!' I had that joy deep within me, a joy that was
different to all the euphoria that sex, drink and drugs had
ever given me. God's joy is not
dependent on external circumstances like the joyous feeling the
world understands. Before this,
my joy would rest upon the money
in my back pocket, a girl on one
arm and a bottle held in the other.
If something threatened any of
those factors, or removed them,
then my feeling of happiness and
joy quickly dissipated. The joy of Jesus is absolutely fantastic. I had years yet to serve at Aylesbury, long days to
languish behind locked doors and barred windows. But
now I really didn't care. I had found the answer to life; I

*O what joy for
those who are
forgiven!*

had discovered what it was that my heart had craved for over all those terrible years. Through that Gideon Bible left on the cell floor, I had made the greatest discovery of my life: one that had given me the greatest joy I had ever known.

The Greatest Discovery

Over the years, millions have discovered that Jesus Christ is the 'Pearl of great price', and when they give all that they have to own him, they possess the greatest treasure in the world.

In the year 1847, a doctor from Edinburgh, Sir James Simpson, discovered that chloroform could be used as an anaesthetic to render people insensible to the pain of surgery. From his early experiments, Dr Simpson made it possible for people to go through the most dangerous operations without fear of pain and suffering. Some people even claim that his was one of the most significant discoveries of modern medicine. Some years later, while lecturing at the University of Edinburgh, Dr Simpson was asked by one of his students, 'What do you consider to be the greatest discovery of your life-

My greatest discovery was when I discovered myself a sinner and that Jesus Christ was my Saviour

time?' To the surprise of his students, who had expected him to refer to chloroform, Dr Simpson replied, 'My greatest discovery was when I discovered myself a sinner and that Jesus Christ was my Saviour.'

I knew that God's presence was with me in my cell. An awesome sense of peace and holiness prevailed, mixed with a deep joy that seemed to bubble up and flow from a well opened up within my heart. Wiping the tears from my face, I grabbed the Bible and finding Matthew 6, gazed at the words of Jesus as he taught the people what we all know as 'The Lord's Prayer'. Using those words I began to pray to God. I voiced my thoughts to God quietly and vocally. Afterwards, I poured out my heartfelt thanks to my Heavenly Father, for now I realised that's who he really is. I had made the greatest discovery any man could make in finding Christ as Saviour. I didn't realise the full extent of my discovery then, but I was later to understand that my new life of faith in Jesus Christ had made me seriously rich. As I climbed into my bed and pulled the green prison blanket over me to keep out the night chill, I knew that my life would never be the same again.

9

SERIOUSLY RICH

The days following my salvation experience were ones of deep joy and wonderful peace. I was indeed a new person and the old things had passed away. My life of waste and ruin had been transformed – now I was seriously rich! The Bible says that *'The blessing of the Lord makes a person rich, and he adds no sorrow with it.'*[16]

And that was my experience. I had found in Jesus Christ true treasure that made me more than a millionaire; treasure that would satisfy my heart and give me a sense of inner joy that the biggest bank account could never buy. Jesus once told a parable about true treasure. *'The Kingdom of Heaven is like a treasure that a man discovered hidden in a field. In his excitement, he hid it again and sold everything he owned to get enough money to buy the field – and to get the treasure, too'!*[17]

I was like that man. I had stumbled over the treasure as I read the pages of the Bible. I realised that my lifestyle had made me poor, but the treasure Jesus Christ offered would make me seriously rich. I just had to own Christ, and so I was glad to sell all I had to possess him. I was only too pleased to give up my wrong lifestyle and perverted sense of values, to get my hands on the treasure of knowing God personally.

Daily, I continued to read my Bible, rejoicing at the
treasures I discovered God had given me to make me rich
through his son Jesus Christ. Yes, Jesus had brought me to

a place of fabulous wealth, a
wealth that has no limit, through
his love and death for us on the
cross. The Apostle Paul taught the
church at Corinth this truth by
saying, '*You know how full of love
and kindness our Lord Jesus Christ
was. Though he was very rich, yet for
your sakes he became poor, so that by
his poverty he could make you rich*'.[18]

*Jesus had brought
me to a place of
fabulous wealth, a
wealth that has no
limit*

I knew I was seriously rich when I began to realise
increasingly that I had a father in heaven who deeply
loved me. I remember reading Isaiah 49 for the first time;
a scripture that speaks about the possibility of a mother
forgetting her child, but God saying that he would never
forget his people. I was amazed when God spoke to me
saying he had engraved my name upon the palms of his
hands. That spoke to me of being unforgettable to God.
People had forgotten Richard Pidgley, a criminal who had
been lost in the prison system, now reduced to a mere
number. My name, however, was ever before my father in
heaven. I was unforgettable to him and, although I was
locked away, I knew that God would remember my plight
as he saw my name engraved upon his hands.

To have my name engraved on God's hands meant that
my new relationship with God was invaluable to him.
Engraving means to cut the image deep into the surface.
If you pick up a trophy you can feel the engraving cut
deep into the surface of the metal. My place in God's
heart was of the utmost importance to him. This new relationship I had with him was no fleeting teenage love

story, but something permanent, just as a name engraved into the surface of a trophy is permanent. That's why the Bible talks about adoption being part of the 'New Birth' experience. *'His unchanging plan has always been to adopt us into his own family by bringing us to himself through Jesus Christ. And this gave him great pleasure.'*[19]

Now, coming from my children's home background, I knew that fostering meant temporary care, and that although the care could be excellent, with all concerned being happy, there could, however, be no lasting security in the relationship. To be fostered meant that at any time you could be snatched away to a new home, whether you wanted it or not. In contrast, to be adopted was different. Once adopted into a family you had the full rights as a legitimate child of the family and the security that you belonged to the adopting parents, and that no cruel system could ever snatch you away from your home.

To be adopted by God was the most wonderful thing that had happened to me! I knew that I was totally secure in his hands and nothing would ever change that. I didn't have to worry that my new-found peace and happiness would be taken from me, because Jesus himself said, *'I give them eternal life, and they will never perish. No one will snatch them away from me, for my Father has given them to me, and he is more powerful than anyone else. So no one can take them from me. The Father and I are one.'*[20]

Billy Bray, the famous Cornish evangelist, who was a rough, hard drinking and sinful man before Christ marvellously saved him, recognised the great implications of his salvation. He, too, was seriously rich and so, when he discovered the wonder of 'adoption', went everywhere telling people with great joy, 'I'm the King's son!'

I knew that I was rich when I discovered the peace of God. For years I had not known much stability of either life or mind, but now I was filled with deep peace. My circumstances were far from peaceful, as the prison doors constantly banged shut on an ever-changing company of convicts, as men came and went. The Bible speaks of God as being our rock; a picture of strength and abiding security. That's what God had become to me now. When king David was relentlessly pursued by his enemies thousands of years ago, he found peace by trusting and abiding in God's presence. David described God as his rock and his fortress, in whom he could find rest and peace for his soul.

God's peace is supernatural and it kept me, in the midst of a very stressful situation. For many, the prison regime with its locked doors, claustrophobic cells and the unending threats of violence from prisoner to prisoner, is stressful. These things cause anxiety and that was something I had suffered from for many years. But now, the outward circumstances no longer troubled me, as, deep inside, God's peace kept my heart and soul in perfect rest. I felt that even if everything around me crumbled away, instead of 'losing it', like I once would have done, I now found myself being kept secure and in a healthy state of mind through the presence of God in my life.

Bible Study

When you have faith in God's Word, the Bible, you are seriously rich! Although nobody came and gave me a basic Bible study in the doctrine of salvation and who God was, I soon grasped the important things through the help of the Holy Spirit. Jesus spoke about the Holy Spirit as our personal Bible teacher whom he would send to all those who believed in him. *'And I will ask the Father, and he will give you another Counsellor, who will never leave you. He is the Holy Spirit, who leads into all truth. The world at large cannot receive him, because it isn't looking for him and doesn't recognise him. But you do, because he lives with you now and later will be in you.'*[21]

To develop a relationship, a couple must spend time together, and I had plenty of time on my hands. After being on A Wing for a few days, I was given a job in one of the prison workshops making 'Zorro' swords and masks. I hated the job, but at least it was better than sewing mailbags, as I had done at Dorchester prison, with eight stitches per inch! Once the work was over, I was escorted with the other prisoners back to the cells. For me this was the best part of the day. As soon as the cell door slammed shut and the automatic lock sprang into place with a loud mechanical click, I would sit on my bed and read my Bible and pray.

A developing relationship needs communication, and the Christian life is all about regular communication between God and us. I believed that the Bible was the Word of God: I never doubted it; I just accepted it by faith. The Apostle Peter, in writing to the early Christian Church, affirmed the genuineness of the Scriptures by saying, *'Above all, you must understand that no prophecy in Scripture ever came from the prophets themselves or because they wanted to prophesy. It was the Holy Spirit who moved the prophets to speak from God.'*[22] In other words, the Bible was not written by men who had too much cheese before sleeping and then awoke the next day saying, 'I think I shall write something for the Bible today.' The Holy Spirit of God moved in their hearts, inspiring them with the revelation of God. This was written down and eventually became the scriptures that have been preserved, in their purity and clarity, by the Holy Spirit, even to this generation. When the Apostle Paul wrote to a young pastor called Timothy he said, *'You have been taught the Holy Scriptures from childhood, and they have given you the wisdom to receive the salvation that comes by trusting in Christ Jesus. All Scripture is inspired by God and is useful to teach us what is true and to make us realise what is wrong in our lives. It straightens us out and teaches us to do what is right. It is God's way of preparing us in every way, fully equipped for every good thing God wants us to do.'*[23]

Paul knew that men had actually written the Bible, or the scriptures, as it was known then. A human hand had scribed patiently all those wonderful life-giving words. But, although a human hand had written the words down, it was the Holy Spirit of God who had given the inspiration. So the Bible is totally written by man, but at the same time, it is also totally inspired by God. For me, this was no problem For some, however, it is a great stumbling block, as they cannot accept the authenticity of the Bible being God's Word for man. The matter must be accepted by faith. Unless we do this, the Bible will be no more than a religious book.

> *The Bible is totally written by man, but at the same time, it is also totally inspired by God*

I listened to God, as he whispered into my heart his deep love and care for me. I also began to hear God's voice speak to me, revealing his plans for my life. I loved nothing more than to read passages of the scripture and then meditate upon them. I would ask myself, 'What is God saying to me?' Then, as I basked in the warmth of God's love, the sunshine of heaven would flood my mind with the light and revelation of Jesus

Christ. I used to skip and dance around my cell when
God spoke to me. I was so excited about my new relationship with God that the concept of being a prisoner in
a Victorian jail didn't bother me. One night, as I read
through the now familiar chapters of Matthew 5–7 and
delighted in Jesus' sermon on the mount, the thought
occurred to me that one day I might be locked in prison
again. This time it would not be for crime, but for the
Gospel's sake, and I ought to begin to memorise the
Scriptures. That was it. From that moment, I determined
to commit the Sermon on the Mount to memory.
Incredible as it seems to me now, I learned those three
golden chapters in one night! Then, every night before I
went to bed, I would pace up and down my little cell
'preaching' one of Jesus' most famous sermons to the thin
air.

Those days in Aylesbury kindled a fire in my heart that
blazes to this very day – a passion for the Bible. I had read
so many demonic books and evil
literature over my short lifetime
and knew that they contained the
power of the kingdom of darkness.
But now, courtesy of The Gideons
International, I had in my hands
the greatest book in the world. The
Bible is the most popular book in
the world; millions of copies are
sold consistently every year.

Now, courtesy of The Gideons International, I had in my hands the greatest book in the world

Yes, the Bible is the most popular and powerful book of
all time and, for millions around the world, it's the most
precious book anyone has ever had the privilege to lay
their hands upon. People have fought and died, giving
their very blood to possess the Holy Scriptures. Others
have been burnt at the stake to preserve the purity of the

Word of God against heresy. There is something about the
Bible that attracts millions of hungry souls to it year by
year. Jesus explained the reason for this, when one day he
found himself in a battle against the devil. Jesus had just
spent forty days of fasting in the wilderness and as you
can well imagine, was feeling very hungry. In the weakness and exhaustion of his flesh the devil came to him and
asked him why, if he was that hungry, he didn't command the very stones at his feet to become bread? Jesus
answered the devil by saying, *'It is written: 'Man does not
live on bread alone, but on every word that comes from the
mouth of God.'*[24]

Once you have tasted the 'living bread' of the Word of
God you will never want to feed upon any thing else. God's
Word satisfied my deep hunger for truth. The entrance of
that truth floodlit the dark recesses of my mind. I had tasted
the truth, and so daily I would 'feed' upon the Word of God,
finding those hours spent in the garden of Scripture my
greatest delight. The Psalmist declared, at the very beginning of the book of Psalms, that the Word of God, or the
'Law of the Lord' as it was known then, was his delight also.
*'Oh, the joys of those who do not follow the advice of the wicked,
or stand around with sinners, or join in with scoffers. But they
delight in doing everything the Lord wants; day and night they
think about his law. They are like trees planted along the riverbank, bearing fruit each season without fail. Their leaves never
wither, and in all they do, they prosper.'*[25]

No longer was I interested in a life of sin; God had
changed all that. Now I was totally dedicated to the Lord
and I delighted in his Law. Just as the psalmist observed,
I began to notice also that I was like *'a tree planted along the
riverbank.'* Where I used to be empty, dry and barren, now
I was flourishing. I was beginning to see the fruit of the
Holy Spirit growing in my life. God's character was being

formed, slowly, steadily, but surely in my life. I was becoming like Jesus. Now that's an awesome thing for anyone, especially a prisoner like me, yet this is the will of God for everyone who trusts in him. *'For God knew his people in advance, and he chose them to become like his Son.'*[26]

Prayer

Communication is not only listening, but talking as well, and prayer is the way we talk to God. Yes, I was rich because I had found a way of talking personally with the God who had created all that is seen and unseen. The first few times I prayed, I was like a child learning to walk, stumbling and falling and then pulling itself up and trying again. Although I knew that some people prayed formally as part of a ritualistic worship service, I saw in the Bible that when people prayed to God it was straight from their hearts. Jesus himself saw prayer as talking with his father in heaven; there was no need to put on an act. It should just be simple and sincere, and flow from a heart that desires to communicate clearly with God. Soon, however, I learned to pray about anything and everything. Jesus taught so much on prayer throughout the Gospels. He encouraged his disciples to pray earnestly by keeping on asking, seeking and knocking. As I began to pray from a sincere heart that was now right with

> *Prayer is as mighty as God Himself, for God Himself has committed Himself to answering prayer*

God, through faith in Jesus Christ, I realised that my father in heaven was actually listening to me. I was amazed to read in my Bible God's wonderful promise to answer our prayers. *'Call upon me and I will answer you.'*[27]

The marvellous truth is this: 'Prayer is as mighty as God himself, for God himself has committed himself to answering prayer.'[28]

I had a promise! I had something I could stand on and believe. God was saying to me, 'Come on and speak to me, I am listening to you.' I guess I felt nobody had listened to me for years, but now I had the ears of God himself listening to my heart's cry. What an incredible thing! The God who sustains all things by the power of his word, has time for each one of us who look to him in faith. I was always a nervous sort of person when it came to speaking up for myself, and would find my lips stuttering in the presence of those who I perceived to be better than myself. Yet now I had discovered the joy of prayer, I could actually talk with God.

The Old Testament teaches us that God's presence was something to be feared and revered as awesome in its glory and holiness. The manifest presence of God was kept from the eyes of the Children of Israel in the tabernacle and then later in the great temple that King Solomon built for God. But this wonderful holy presence of God was not only kept from the Israelite people, but even from the priests who ministered to God by worship and sacrifices. The manifest presence of God was reserved for the Most Holy Place; this small area, which was set aside from the rest of the tabernacle – and later the temple – as the most special holy place anyone could ever enter. In fact, it was so holy and awesome that the high priest could only minister in God's presence there once a year. The people would hold their breath as the high priest entered the Most Holy Place to minister to the Lord. They knew all too well that some had encountered God's holiness in the past with wrong hearts, and because of their sin they perished.

Prayer in the Holy Place was something very special, and reserved for the few select high priests who had served throughout the generations. But the glorious truth is this: I, as a forgiven sinner, can enter the Most Holy Place. By faith in Jesus' work upon the cross, I have an access to the Holy of Holies and I can speak with the eternal Monarch of the universe. I hadn't long been saved from my sins and I didn't know much theology, but I had read the Bible for myself and, in reading those blessed pages, light dawned upon my soul that I had the right, as a son, to approach my heavenly father. The Bible puts it like this: *'And so, dear brothers and sisters, we can boldly enter heaven's Most Holy Place because of the blood of Jesus. This is the new, life-giving way that Christ has opened up for us through the sacred curtain, by means of his death for us.'*[29]

Now that's serious wealth! I read a story some time ago, from American history, which illustrates this glorious truth.

'There was once a soldier in the Union Army, a young man who had lost his older brother and father in the war. He went to Washington DC to see President Lincoln to ask for an exemption from military service so that he could go back and help his sister and mother with the spring planting on their farm. When the young soldier arrived in Washington . . . he went to the White House, approached the doors, and asked to see the President. [He was told, however, that he could not see the president as he was too busy and that he should go back and fight the rebels]. So he left, very disheartened, and was sitting on a little park bench not far from the White House when a little boy came up to him. The lad said, 'Soldier, you look unhappy. What's wrong?' The soldier looked at the young boy and began to spill his heart out to this young lad about his situation, about his father and his brother having died in the war, and how he was the only male left in the family and was needed desperately back at the farm for the spring planting.

'The little boy took the soldier by the hand and led him around the back of the White House. They went through the back door, past the guards, past all the generals and high ranking government officials until they got to the President's office itself. The little boy didn't even knock on the door but just opened it and walked in. There was President Lincoln, with his Secretary of State, looking over battle plans on the desk. President Lincoln looked up and said, "What can I do for you Todd?" And Todd replied, "Father, this soldier needs to talk with you." Right there and then the young soldier had his chance to plead his case with President Lincoln, and he was exempted from military service due to the hardship his family was under.'[30]

> *It is the Son who brings us to the Father's throne and says, 'Father there is someone here to talk with you'*

Such is the case with the ascended Lord Jesus. You see, we too, have access to the Father through the Son. It is the Son who brings us to the Father's throne and says, 'Father there is someone here to talk with you.'

As the days rolled on, I was excited as I saw that God was answering my prayers. Sometimes God answered in the way I thought he would. Other times, God would answer me in a far greater way than I could ever have hoped or dreamed. I also discovered that not everything was good for me, or God's will for me; so in loving kindness and infinite wisdom, God simply said, 'No!'

Rapid Promotion

I was in my cell during one lunchtime lock-up period, reading my Bible, when the cell door opened. Standing in the doorway was the senior officer from the prison kitchen dressed in 'whites'. He asked me a few questions about my butchery experience and, although I answered every question correctly, I could see that he wasn't convinced. The SO (senior officer) asked me to follow him to the kitchen to do a 'block test', which was a practical exam. It turned out that the prison butcher had been sacked for some misdemeanour and the kitchen crew of about fifteen men were helpless, because none of them had any butchery experience.

The kitchen was half empty when we got there, as some of the lads were not needed during the lunch-break period. The kitchen area was massive compared to what I was accustomed to, and the feeling of space was fantastic. The SO pointed to the block, on which lay a whole pig! I was given a white coat, some butcher's knives and a saw and told to get on with the job. After months of being banged up, this was too good to be true! Within minutes, the whole pig was skilfully cut and prepared for cooking, with the legs boned and rolled for roasting and the belly and loin chopped and laid neatly out on meat trays.

I knocked on the office door adjoining the kitchen and went in saying, 'J52327 Pidgley, Sir'. Well, things were looking up, because they told me it was more relaxed in the prison kitchen and I didn't have to report like that there. The SO came out and looked at my handiwork and was impressed: so impressed, in fact, that I got the job instantly!

Talk about rapid promotion, it was incredible. The kitchen jobs were regarded as the best jobs in the whole prison for their many benefits. The coveted kitchen jobs

paid well. The salary I received, as the one and only
skilled butcher, was the prison's top pay! Overnight, I
had overtaken the pay structure of every other prisoner at
Aylesbury. Now that was a great blessing to me. Those
working in the kitchen got extra clean sets of clothing
every week and a shower every day. We were also out of
our prison cells each day for longer than all the other prisoners. While on duty in the kitchen, every worker could
pretty well eat what they liked, and I would regularly cut
steaks for the lads to grill.

I also discovered how rich I was when I realised that God
had many other children, which made them spiritually my
brothers and sisters. Fellowship is one of the most precious
gifts we have in the Church. God never intended any
Christian to play 'the Lone Ranger'. Rather, he places us
into the Christian Family. It is possible to be a Christian and
not go to church, and there are some people who, due to
exceptional circumstances, have no fellowship. Terry Waite,
the well-known British hostage was kept in isolation for
years. However, able-bodied Christians who don't attend
church services or fellowship with other believers, are missing God's best for them. The writer to the Hebrews spells
this out clearly. *'And let us not neglect our meeting together, as
some people do, but encourage and warn each other, especially
now that the day of his coming back again is drawing near.'*[31]

We need the encouragement of other like-minded
Christians, so meeting for fellowship, to pray, to worship
and share the scriptures together is vital for our spiritual
health. The Apostle Paul was on a missionary trip once to
Corinth, and I guess he felt a bit lonely, so God graciously
spoke to him alleviating his fears. *'One night the Lord spoke
to Paul in a vision and told him, "Don't be afraid! Speak out!
Don't be silent! For I am with you, and no one will harm you
because many people here in this city belong to me." '*[32]

The Lord knew that I needed friendship and brought into my life at Aylesbury two men who would prove to be true and wonderful Christian brothers. Grant and Kris, both young men, had very recently become Christians themselves. Because of a lack of encouragement, they were silent about their new-found faith, but once I joined them on the prison kitchen crew they 'came out' and joined me in being open about their faith. Grant and Kris also knew the wonder of salvation in a special way, for both of them had the blood of murder upon their hands and were sentenced 'to be detained at her Majesty's Pleasure', which is the youth equivalent to an adult 'Life Sentence'. These young men had already served about six years of their lives behind bars. Although they had such a long way to go, they too were really free: gloriously set free from the kingdom of darkness that had held them captive as young men and caused them to be incarcerated for the crime of murder.

Our friendship blossomed behind the bars of Aylesbury Youth Custody Centre. We were totally honest with each other and stood up for each other when things got tough. This time, however, it was not a case of resorting to flesh and blood, which had resulted in us being in prison in the first place, but by praying fervently for one another. We would sit on Grant's bed often, while the doors on the wing were open, and snatch precious times together, praying and reading the scriptures. Although we didn't realise it at the time, we had our own church meetings that were full of faith and heartfelt worship. Jesus, desiring his people to meet in honour of him, once said about such gatherings, *'For where two or three gather together because they are mine, I am there among them.'*[33]

What times of rejoicing we had as we sang God's praises and revelled in his love for us. We were sincere in our

fellowship together and, because of the deep love that we
had for each other, we found that our times of worship were
attracting other people to Jesus. The prisoners noted that
we had something that was real. There are many fair-
weather friends in prison who can't be trusted, and so,
when they saw in us the joy of true Christian fellowship,
they wanted it as well. They saw that they were spiritually
poor and that we were spiritually rich, and they wanted
what we had too. Our gatherings in the cell got too big and
the chaplain eventually put on an afternoon Bible Study
just for us, to accommodate the growing church.

Persecution

Not long after I started working in the prison kitchen, I
came up against my first test of how strong my new-
found faith really was. Sunday morning was Chapel
Service for any of the men who wanted to go along.
Usually, the chapel would be crowded, not with worship-
pers, but with convicts who longed to be free from their
cells for the length of time it took to go through the
Anglican Eucharist Service. Those working in the
kitchens were allowed to attend the service, but had to
give their name to the SO before breakfast so that they
had provision for an officer to escort them to the service
and bring them back again to the kitchen.

In the butcher's room, which also housed the refriger-
ators for the rest of the kitchen, about twelve men had
gathered and were talking after breakfast. The men were
giving one of the lads a hard time because they had discovered that he wanted to go to the church service that
morning. The debate was pretty heated as the men
argued about the existence of God and why we should
worship him. As I walked into the room, I could see that

the lad who went to church was having a hard time. When he finally gave up the fight, I stepped in and began to explain that worship was a natural response to the God who loved us and gave himself for us upon the cross. I didn't realise it at the time, but I had preached my first Gospel sermon just weeks after being converted! I spoke at length on the power of the Cross, and how the blood of Christ could wash away even the bloodstained guilt of murder. The men were gripped and listened to every word that came from my mouth. When I finally finished, they quietly got on with their jobs. Nobody spoke a word as the Holy Spirit began to do a work in them that would change some of their lives, just as mine had been transformed.

The next day, Winston, a black man, called me into the vegetable preparation bay for a chat. I remember feeling cautious about this, because this man was all muscle. He stood taller than me, and every muscle in his body was rippling as he spent hours of his free time in the prison gym doing weight-lifting and circuit-training. To say that he looked like a black version of Arnold Schwarzenegger was no exaggeration! The man was a lean, mean, fighting machine, and was held in great awe by all the other cons.

With a dry throat and a sense of menace, I approached Winston, only to find my exit from that preparation bay was blocked by about five of the other prisoners who knew what was coming. Winston began to talk, telling me that he hated Christians and would have nothing to do with God. He said that he didn't approve of preachers and hoped that I would never try to convert him, because if I did, he would have to teach me a lesson. Then the crunch came, as he asked me if God loved him. Without thinking, I opened my mouth and said, 'Winston, God hates the sin that controls your life, but he loves you so much that he sent Jesus to die on the cross for you so you can be set free.' The next moment I was wiping blood from my mouth, as a fist that felt like a black iron, crashed

> *God hates the sin that controls your life, but he loves you so much that he sent Jesus to die on the cross for you so you can be set free*

into my face. Just months before, if I'd had a knife in my hand, I would have thrust it deep into his abdomen, spilling his entrails upon the kitchen floor. Now, something had changed within me. The old me who would have hated and despised this black man, felt only love and compassion for him. Winston, disgusted at the lack of retaliation, spat at me and pushed me to one side, and his entourage followed him, leaving me alone.

That night, once again, I found myself reading the 'Sermon on the mount'. When I read the passage on persecution, Jesus' words burned deep within my heart. *'God blesses you when you are mocked and persecuted and lied about because you are my followers. Be happy about it! Be very glad! For a great reward awaits you in heaven. And remember, the ancient prophets were persecuted, too.'*[34]

As strange as it seemed, I was blessed for that encounter with Winston earlier in the day. In fact, Jesus was saying, be glad and realise that you are in good company, because great heroes of faith, who have stood for the truth before you, have suffered also. Jesus was saying to me, 'It's tough now, but wait till you see the great reward in heaven I've laid on for you!' I began to praise God that I was counted worthy to suffer for the Gospel's sake, just as the Early Church did hundreds of years ago, when they were beaten by the Jewish religious leaders for proclaiming Jesus as the answer to mankind's sin. I must admit, my mouth was still sore and my lip was puffed up from the sudden impact of Winston's fist. I was blessed, yes, but I wasn't looking to be blessed like that again for a long while! However, as I read on, I saw something else that Jesus said, and this time I wasn't so excited. '*You have heard that the law of Moses says, 'If an eye is injured, injure the eye of the person who did it. If a tooth gets knocked out, knock out the tooth of the person who did it.' But I say, don't resist an evil person! If you are slapped on the right cheek, turn the other, too.'*[35]

The Bible told me I was blessed if I was persecuted, and also instructed me what to do when persecuted – turn the other cheek! That's tough teaching for a young convert, particularly when you want to save face before everyone else in the kitchen. The next month, I learned much about grace and prayer! Day after day, Winston would question me about my faith. He would ask about Jesus and his power to transform lives. He would ask about the power of Jesus' blood to remove sin. He would ask about forgiveness and peace with God. And, sure enough at the end of the interrogations, he would ask me if Jesus loved him. Every time, I answered him by saying 'Yes'. Sometimes the result was the excruciating pain of a boot aimed at my genitals, other times the blood would trickle down from my nose or mouth.

Whatever came, I received grace to endure it. In fact, I grew stronger in my faith, and the daily sport of seeing me receive such beatings from Winston began to have a strange effect on the other cons in the kitchen. When Winston was out of the way they would listen for ages as I told them all I knew of the Good Shepherd who

What had started as cruel bullying was being turned into a powerful demonstration of God's grace and immense love for these young men

gave his life for us. I rejoiced before the Lord every night, as I prayed for Winston and the other lads. What had started as cruel bullying was being turned into a powerful demonstration of God's grace and immense love for these young men. I pleaded with the Lord to save Winston and the others, and thanked him for a message of hope to give them daily, in spite of the beatings.

One day, about a month after Winston first questioned me about the Gospel, my face and body bruised with all the daily punishment of violence, I was summoned once again at lunchtime into the bakery area of the kitchen. This time there was one convict and Winston. As I braced myself for the inevitable beating, Winston began to ask searching questions about the love of Christ. Ready for the fist of pain to strike my face, I told Winston that Jesus loved him so very much and desired more than anything else that he should turn from his sin and give his life to him. The fist never struck me. As I looked up, I saw the tears streaming down Winston's face and falling upon the hard floor. Quietly he said, 'I want to give my life to this Jesus who you say loves me.' Fighting back the tears, I reached out my hand and clasped it upon his shoulder. (This would have normally brought the death sentence to anyone else!) Dragging Winston to his knees with me, there and then, on that kitchen floor, I led this hard man of violence to Christ. That night, I wept with joy before the Lord. I knew then that Jesus was going to use me to bring others to him. I began to pray fervently for souls, from that time on. I called out to Jesus saying, 'Lord, you said if I follow you, you will make me a fisher of men.' A sense of mission was born in my heart, and I felt the compelling driving force of God's love burden my heart for those languishing in cells all around me.

The prison community held its breath a few months later when, one night, during a special service in the chapel, the Bishop of Oxford confirmed Winston and me. A stronghold had been broken as one of the prison's toughest had bowed his knees to Christ. If God could save Winston, then he could save anyone. The lessons of perseverance, prayer and grace through the persecution, taught me much for the days of soul winning that lay ahead of me before my release from Aylesbury.

> *A stronghold had been broken as one of the prison's toughest had bowed his knees to Christ*

Margaret

For most of my captivity, I hadn't seen anyone during the allocated prison visits to which I was entitled. The Governor issues every convict a visiting order (or VO) at least once a month, or more often, depending on the prison. I had nobody to visit me at Aylesbury and, because I had got used to the fact that there were going to be no visits, I didn't worry about it. One day, however, Philip, the chaplain, asked me if I would like a visit from a lady who attended the local Anglican church on the estate just round the corner from the prison. With nothing to lose, I agreed.

So, sure enough, on the next visiting day I was called from working in the kitchen and escorted by an officer to the visiting room. Once I had been searched for anything that was considered illegal in prison, such as drugs or letters and even plans of the prison for a possible escape attempt, I was allowed to go into the room. When I entered the visiting room I was shown to a desk where a

middle-aged lady was sitting, patiently waiting. I guess
neither of us was sure of what to expect, and so the first
few minutes seemed hard. But Margaret, sensing my shy-
ness, smiled and began to ask me questions about myself,
and how I had become a Christian. Once we started to
talk about God, I relaxed, because I then realised that
Margaret was not concerned about my past, but keen to
be a friend and sister to me in the present. We had never
met before that day, but after that first half-hour visit, I
felt such warmth and love from Margaret that I was only
too pleased when she asked if I would like her to come in
again. Just before the visit ended, she asked if she could
pray for me. I agreed, and Margaret reached out her hand
and, gently holding mine, began to pray for me that God
would bless and protect me and fill me with a joy and
knowledge of himself. The visit over, I waved goodbye to
Margaret as they took me to the door and frisked me for
any contraband.

That night, I sat on my bed in the cell and began to
thank God for Margaret and her family, whom I had
heard a little about earlier in the day. I couldn't get over
the love and great acceptance that Margaret had given
me. Here I was, a prisoner doing time for all the rotten
things I had done, but this woman was prepared to come
and visit me and talk to me about the wonder of God. Yes,
that night, as I went to sleep, once again, I thanked God
for making me seriously rich.

The fortnightly visits by Margaret were the highlight
of my life at that time. We sat for many hours over the
following months talking about the Lord. I told
Margaret about the different needs all around me in my
world of locks and bars. She would take me through the
scriptures and lovingly give me the wisdom of God to
cope with everything thrown at a young Christian. I

don't know if I ever showed enough appreciation to
Margaret for those hours she spent with me: her sacrifice
of time and energy to make a disciple out of a young
man. Years on, I realise that she did so much. She taught
me to pray for other people's needs by intercession. She
explained the world of spiritual warfare that helped me
cope with the gross darkness of prison life. She constantly reminded me of Paul's revelation to the church in
Ephesus when they struggled with the opposition of
their day. Paul wrote to them saying, *'A final word: Be
strong with the Lord's mighty power. Put on all of God's
armour so that you will be able to stand firm against all
strategies and tricks of the Devil. For we are not fighting
against people made of flesh and blood, but against the evil
rulers and authorities of the unseen world, against those
mighty powers of darkness who rule this world, and against
wicked spirits in the heavenly realms.'*[36]

Margaret helped me understand that often it was the
satanic powers of darkness behind difficult situations.
This meant I could be free to love the individuals who
caused problems in the prison and pray against the powers that held them captive.

I guess if you asked Margaret today what my theology
and doctrine were like in those early days, she would
have to tell you I had some 'interesting' ideas! But she
was so patient, and lovingly listened to me and gently
corrected me, steering me into solid doctrine that would
be the basis of a healthy and wonderful Christian life.
Margaret bought me a Bible, as a present, that would be
my own. I still have it today and often pick it up from my
study bookshelf and remember those precious times
when we looked into its pages together in that visiting
room, rejoicing in the great truths of God's infinite wisdom and eternal love for us.

The great thing about Christianity is, not only do you discover that the God of the universe adopts you as his own child, but also that you are added to a great family! In fact, it's the greatest family in the world, with members in almost every nation. I have found such love in the Church worldwide. Once, when visiting South Africa, my family and I were treated like long-lost relatives who had just turned up. The members of the local church we visited in Cape Town welcomed us into their homes and accepted us as their own, even though they had never seen us before and we had travelled half the way around the world to be there. Before I became a Christian, I knew first-hand the plight of the lonely and the rejected, but now I was accepted and loved by people whom I had just met. They were family because we all had the same heavenly father. How true the Bible was in describing my new status: *'God places the lonely in families; he sets the prisoners free and gives them joy.'*[37]

Margaret and her husband John, along with their daughters, embraced me for what I was now and not what I used to be. They all recognised the grace of God and the forgiveness that was mine in Christ. This beautiful family warmly welcomed me, without any suspicion, into their lives. For that love and welcome, I am eternally grateful. This loving family from Aylesbury had taught me so much about practical love and a genuine Christian lifestyle, without any trappings of hypocrisy.

This beautiful family warmly welcomed me, without any suspicion, into their lives. For that love and welcome, I am eternally grateful

Yes, the blessing of God makes us rich. I am so thankful for the day I discovered the field with its treasure. Yes, I had to give up my old way of living to gain the treasure, but it was worth it. God replaced my old ruined and wasted life with the fabulous treasure of a whole new life, knowing Jesus Christ as my Saviour. He became poor so that, through his poverty, I might become seriously rich.

10

SIGNS AND WONDERS

The Holy Spirit

On the night of the 14th March 1985, as I sat alone in my cell, I had an amazing experience. It had all started at the chaplain's hour earlier that day, held in the prison chapel. The meeting had been led by Margaret and her friend Jill, a member of Margaret's church. We sang some worship songs and then had a Bible study that Margaret had prepared from Acts 19. We were reading that day all about the people of Ephesus, who had turned to Christ for salvation and were now renouncing their occult dealings by publicly burning their magic books as they chose to serve God and wholeheartedly follow him. I can remember saying to the Lord that I, too, would have done what the saints at Ephesus did with their occult things, if I'd had a bonfire. I sat on my bed and read from my Bible, Psalm 51. This passage of scripture referred to the time the prophet Nathan came to King David and confronted him with his sin of adultery and murder. King David, in penitence, cried out to God, *'Have mercy on me, O God, because of your unfailing love. Because of your great compassion, blot out the stain of my sins. Wash me clean from my guilt. Purify me from my sin.'*[38]

Although I knew that every sin I had ever committed had been forgiven by a gracious, loving heavenly father and that the blood of Jesus Christ had totally washed me clean, I felt that somehow I still needed to specifically get the 'occult sins' off my chest, and renounce them vocally, loud and clear for God and the devil to hear once and for all. I prayed that God would have mercy on me also. I remember being truly sorry for every single occult activity in which I had ever been foolish enough to be involved. As I read King David's heart-cry of deep repentance to God, the words sank into my heart. *'Unseal my lips, O Lord, that I may praise you. You would not be pleased with sacrifices, or I would bring them. If I brought you a burnt offering, you would not accept it. The sacrifice you want is a broken spirit. A broken and repentant heart, O God, you will not despise.'*[39]

Then, as I sat on my bed with my Bible in my hand, suddenly the glory of God came upon me. A strange, glorious fire seemed to engulf me, and yet it didn't burn me. I could feel the sensation of flickering flames all over me; but I couldn't feel any searing heat or pain, just great joy. Tears of joy were streaming down my cheeks as I bathed in God's awesome presence. The experience was like nothing I had ever known before. I sank from the bed to my knees and lifted my hands to heaven, in total worship and abandonment to God.

Suddenly the glory of God came upon me

As my heart was leaping for joy, my mind was also praising God and then, suddenly, to my surprise, a whole new language came gushing out of my mouth! It was a language I had never spoken nor even heard before, yet I felt comfortable with it, as I was sure I was praising God.

This awesome experience must have gone on for a couple of hours. I was still praising God on my knees as the prison officer came around at 10 p.m. to switch off the lights. As I climbed into bed, I didn't want to stop the new language. It kept flowing. Then it dawned on me that this experience was the same as the apostles and the early church believers had received when they had been filled with the Holy Spirit all those years before. The next day, as I read my Bible, the Holy Spirit led me through the Scriptures, highlighting verses that spoke about the wonder and purpose of being filled with his power.

I was convinced that what I had received was a genuine gift from God. So, armed with this revelation, I went to find my two friends, Grant and Kris. As the three of us sat together in Grant's cell with our Bibles open, I explained to them my experience of the night before. On showing them the scriptures that spoke of the baptism in the Holy Spirit, they, too, believed and asked God for the gift. As we bowed our heads in prayer, I prayed for my two Christian friends and, instantly, they too, spoke in a whole new language that they had never learned before, by the power of the Holy Spirit. What a fantastic time we had, praising God in what the Bible refers to as 'tongues',[40] as the glory of God fell once more upon that prison block in Aylesbury Youth Custody Centre.

The next day I wrote to Margaret, hardly containing my excitement about the experience I had just had. What the prison officer who censored the outgoing letters thought, I don't know. I didn't care, as I felt I could shout from the rooftops God's praises for all to hear! Because of the lack of teaching, I didn't realise that speaking in 'tongues' was something I could quietly practise before the Lord everyday of my life. After those first two wonderful days, like someone who gets over the excitement of a gift and places it away out of sight, I, too, allowed the gift to rest at the back of my mind. When Margaret came in to see me a few days later, she was very excited for me. When I told her that I hadn't spoken in 'tongues' since, she patiently took me through the scriptures that explain the wonder of the 'gift of tongues'. Margaret told me that every time I spoke in 'tongues' I was building myself up spiritually in the Lord. The Apostle Paul spent much time explaining the value of 'spiritual gifts' to the church at Corinth in his first letter to them. Paul knew the value of having this amazing gift and told the believers, '*A person who speaks in tongues is strengthened personally in the Lord*.'[41]

Margaret also told me that when I prayed in 'tongues', the Holy Spirit was helping me to speak to God in a way that bypassed my intellect. And, let's face it, our mind often gets in the way when we think of supernatural things. The Bible puts it this way: '*And the Holy Spirit helps us in our distress. For we don't even know what we should pray for, nor how we should pray. But the Holy Spirit prays for us with groanings that cannot be expressed in words*'.[42]

Now, for me this was a great help, as I wasn't a prayer warrior, and praying was still relatively new to me. I found, as I sought the face of God, that I would often get frustrated, as I wanted to pray a blessing upon someone or some situation and words of intellect failed me. It was then that I would automatically begin to pray in 'tongues' and feel a tremendous burst of faith explode from deep within. When I finished praying about a situation in 'tongues', I had a wonderful sense of God's peace and joy: a feeling that God had heard the prayer and was dealing with it according to his good will and pleasure.

In those early days of great spiritual discovery, I am so glad that Margaret not only encouraged me to seek the blessing of 'spiritual gifts', but that she also kept my feet on the ground, with a gentle and loving wisdom that flows from above. It would have been easy to have been caught up in the power of God and missed out on the grace of God and the fruit that his Spirit brings into our lives. The gifts Margaret told me about were for building up the whole church and not individual personalities. The fruit, however, was to let the beauty of Jesus be seen in me. I could have so easily gone off the rails spiritually, but Margaret was there, always with the Bible and a verse

Let love be your highest goal

that would speak into my situation and give me guidance from God himself. I knew then, as I began to taste the incredible power of the Holy Spirit in my life, that love was more important than all the signs and wonders I would begin to see on an ever increasing scale in my life. That was the wisdom Paul gave the

Corinthian church, as they got all out of balance with the power gifts of the Holy Spirit. He said, *'Let love be your highest goal, but also desire the special abilities the Spirit gives, especially the gift of prophecy.'*[43]

Grant, Kris and I got together and held a small Bible study one night during association time. While the other prisoners watched the telly, we sat in a corner with open Bibles, and read all we could about the Holy Spirit of God and this experience we had all received. We rejoiced when we read the words of John the Baptist who told us, through the pages of time, that Jesus was the baptiser in the Holy Spirit and that what we had experienced was the promise of God. *'I baptise with water those who turn from their sins and turn to God. But someone is coming soon who is*

*far greater than I am – so much greater that I am not even wor-
thy to be his slave. He will baptise you with the Holy Spirit and
with fire.'*[44]

We also knew that when Peter preached his famous
first sermon on the day of Pentecost, he told the crowds
that if they turned to Christ and were baptised in the
name of Jesus, they, too, would receive the Holy Spirit as
the gift of God. Peter stressed that the gift was to all who
came to faith, even those far off, which takes in the whole
length and breadth of humanity, even to this very day.[45]

As we read the New Testament, a new understanding
dawned on us all: the Holy Spirit had not just come
upon us so that we could speak in 'tongues', as fantastic
as that was, but also for other important reasons. We
realised that the baptism of the Holy Spirit was to bring
us into great joy, to strengthen us
for Christian service, and to help
us in our daily walk with the
Lord. The indwelling Spirit was
forming a reproduction of God's
character – 'fruit' – in us. We
looked at each other in awe, as we
read the scripture where Jesus
spoke about the coming Holy
Spirit, just before he went back

*When the Holy
Spirit has come
upon you, you will
receive power*

into heaven. *'But when the Holy Spirit has come upon you,
you will receive power and will tell people about me everywhere
– in Jerusalem, throughout Judea, in Samaria, and to the ends
of the earth.'*[46]

We fully understood this incredible statement – that
the glorious power of God was actually in us to energise
us and equip us for the work of the ministry that he had
commissioned his Church to do. We knew that within us
was the power of God – the same power that raised Jesus

from the dead. The potential for a life that was wholly submitted to the will of God was unlimited! As we prayed together that night, we praised God for what he had entrusted to us, and counted ourselves truly blessed to have been filled with the promised Holy Spirit.

We began to talk with others who we had led to the Lord and told them all about the baptism in the Holy Spirit. Some were not sure but, for those who were eager to have the same experience as the apostles and the Early Church, we told them that they needed to understand that the promise was for them. '*As many as the Lord calls*'[47] the scripture said, and that included converted and forgiven convicts such as us. We showed them a scripture that had blessed us in our little Bible study a few nights before, about when Jesus was speaking to a large crowd at the end of a feast week at the temple in Jerusalem. '*On the last day, the climax of the festival, Jesus stood and shouted to the crowds, "If you are thirsty, come to me! If you believe in me, come and drink! For the Scriptures declare that rivers of living water will flow out from within." (When he said "living water," he was speaking of the Spirit, who would be given to everyone believing in him. But the Spirit had not yet been given, because Jesus had not yet entered into his glory.)*'[48]

Our advice to all those seeking the baptism of the Holy Spirit was simple, and I continue to give it today: 'follow Christ's guidance.' Thirst for the Holy Spirit, and have a desire, deep within, to receive God's gift for all the right reasons. Some people want to speak in 'tongues' only as a sign that they have been there and got the tee shirt! Sadly, such people speak in 'tongues' but never progress in their spiritual life, because inwardly the hunger and thirst for God is not a passionate thing for them. When the passion of your heart is to be filled with more of God, then you must come, by faith, to Jesus. John the Baptist said, '*He will baptise you in the Holy Ghost and with fire!'*[49] In the days of the Early Church, the New Testament records, that some people were helped to be filled with the Holy Spirit when hands were laid on them in prayer. However, ultimately, we must understand that it is Christ who bestows this wonderful gift upon his followers. The simple truth is, once we fulfil these prerequisites, all we have to do is drink by faith. Then, what has been a blessing for millions and is totally in accordance with sound doctrine, can be your experience, too.

As I met other Christians, who were emerging from every wing and landing in the prison, I would lovingly and gently challenge them with the Apostle Paul's question to the believers he found, first at Ephesus, while on a missionary journey: *'Did you receive the Holy Spirit when you believed?'*[50]

Some of the men questioned whether or not it was the will of God to be filled with the Holy Spirit? On searching the scriptures, we found the clear answer one day, when we read Paul's letter to the Church at Ephesus. *'Don't be drunk with wine, because that will ruin your life. Instead, let the Holy Spirit fill and control you. Then you will sing psalms and hymns and spiritual songs among yourselves, making music to the Lord in your hearts. And you will always give thanks for everything to God the Father in the name of our Lord Jesus Christ.'*[51]

For the small 'church' behind the bars of Aylesbury YCC – for that's what we were in God's sight – the answer was absolutely crystal clear. The baptism in the Holy Spirit was for all Christians. It was the command of God that we should each seek to be filled with the Spirit for God's glory. We didn't question the matter after that, but simply prayed daily to be overflowing with the living water, so that our blessings would run onto the dry and thirsty ground of the broken hearts all around us.

After I was filled with the Holy Spirit, things got exciting. It seemed that the scriptures burned with an ever-increasing passion in my heart. As I read about Jesus giving his great commission to the disciples to preach the Gospel to everyone, I too, felt the strong conviction that Christ was talking directly to me. The end of Mark's Gospel was probably the first portion of scripture I ever underlined in the new Bible that Margaret had given me just a few weeks beforehand: *'And then he told them, 'Go into all the world and preach the Good News to everyone, everywhere. Anyone who believes and is baptised will be saved. But anyone who refuses to believe will be condemned. These signs will accompany those who believe: They will cast out demons in my name, and they will speak new languages. They will be able to handle snakes with safety, and if they drink anything poisonous, it won't hurt them. They will be able to place their hands on the sick and heal them.' When the Lord Jesus had finished talking with them, he was taken up into heaven and sat down in the place of honour at God's right hand. And the disciples went everywhere and preached, and the Lord worked with them, confirming what they said by many miraculous signs.'*[52]

The Great Commission of Christ stirred my heart and I knew I had a job to do in the prison. I had already led a few men to faith in Jesus Christ and as wonderful as that was, I knew that they were just the first fruits. I found, as I witnessed to prisoners and officers alike, that I grew bolder, and God helped me marvellously to explain the Gospel from many different angles to a diversity of human misery and heartbreaking needs.

I had a message for the murderer, the rapist, the violent, the depraved: in fact, God gave me a relevant word for each type of convict, and as I spoke with the deep passion of my heart, these men listened. It was glorious to see men coming to Christ, just as I had done earlier.

Aylesbury housed some of the most heinous youth offenders of the nation at that time, and some of them became Christians as I prayed for them and talked with them about the new life Jesus offers us all.

The scripture at the end of Mark's Gospel clearly said, *'and the Lord worked with'* those early Christians as they faithfully preached the Gospel of Jesus Christ. I found, to my joy, that God had not changed, got tired or even retired from what he had begun to do through his people, the Church. As I was praying one day in my cell for the other prisoners, I found myself asking God to confirm the message I had for them with signs and wonders.

> *Jesus Christ is the same yesterday, today, and forever*

I opened my Bible at the book of Hebrews and read a verse that was going to catapult me into a new realm of faith and trust in God: *'Jesus Christ is the same yesterday, today, and forever.'*[53]

The phrase dropped from my mind into my heart and caused me to leap around my cell rejoicing! This mighty Jesus of the New Testament, who had performed all the wonderful miracles that astonished thousands, was able to do exactly the same today. With him, all things were possible, nothing was too hard for him. One day, a man brought his demon-possessed son to Jesus for deliverance, explaining to him, *'The evil spirit often makes him fall into the fire or into water, trying to kill him. Have mercy on us and help us. Do*

> *Jesus is the Saviour, Healer, Baptiser in the Holy Spirit and the mighty coming King. Nothing, absolutely nothing is too hard for Him!*

something if you can.' Jesus replied, *'What do you mean 'If I can'?*[54]

Of course he can! Jesus is the Saviour, Healer, Baptiser in the Holy Spirit and the mighty coming King. Nothing, absolutely nothing is too hard for him!

Healing

A few days later, this text was put to the test. Charlie was a lad from Singapore, who had very foolishly been caught up in smuggling heroin into Britain. He was arrested at the airport and sentenced to eight years' imprisonment. Unfortunately, it didn't end there. The Singapore authorities had notified him that, on his eventual return to Singapore, he would be sentenced to death by hanging for bringing shame upon his nation.

I remember thinking that Charlie was really a convict on death row. The weight of the death sentence hanging over him was like a cloud of darkness. Grant came with me one day and talked with Charlie in the prison kitchen during the lunchtime lock-up period. As we sat in the butcher's room, we explained to Charlie the hope that we had in Christ, and how Jesus could save him from his sins and give him peace and joy. When we asked him if he would like to pray with us and give his heart to the Lord, he readily agreed and, once again, we saw the wonder of another trophy of God's grace emerge from death to life. Although he was a man still living under the sentence of death, the fear of 'hanging until he was pronounced dead' no longer worried him. His soul was right with God, and that is the important issue that everyone must face in this lifetime before it's too late.

Charlie came along to our little Bible studies during lunchtimes and would also pray with us, as often as we could find a quiet corner in the kitchen or cellblock and bow our heads together. One morning, Charlie didn't turn up for work in the kitchen. When we went to his cell the door was locked and he said he felt unwell. During the lunchtime lock-up, Grant and I slipped out of the kitchen and went back to Charlie's cell. Looking through the spy lens in the door, we spoke to him inside. The doctor had been in to see him and had said that he had some skin disease, which he wasn't sure about and, therefore, he would have to go to Stoke Mandeville Hospital to be diagnosed properly and, if possible, treated accordingly. When we asked him how bad it was, Charlie turned his back to us and lifted up his tee shirt to expose a back that was red raw and severely inflamed. I knew then that God could heal this man. The phrase *'Jesus Christ is the same yesterday, today, and forever'* came to my mind powerfully, and I sensed that the Lord was telling Grant and me to pray with Charlie for his healing. I asked him if he believed that Jesus Christ could make him well. When he answered, 'yes', I explained to him that we couldn't lay hands on him because of the locked door, but if he would put his hands on the door his side, we would do the same our side, which was the best we could do. As I prayed with sincere faith, I simply asked God to heal the skin disease on Charlie's back in the name of Jesus Christ. After saying goodbye to Charlie, we quietly crept back into the kitchen before anyone noticed that we had gone.

The very next morning I was in the kitchen at 6.30 a.m. preparing the rashers of bacon that had to be cooked for the prisoners' breakfast. Suddenly, I heard a voice singing a well-known Christian song, 'Majesty'.[55] I turned around from the oven door and was delighted to see Charlie waltzing into the main kitchen. The officer on duty asked him why he hadn't gone to Stoke Mandeville the night before, and Charlie lifted up his tee shirt, exposing a muscular back of healthy skin. 'Jesus healed me!' he said as he continued to sing 'Majesty'. The healing power of God was the talking point of the day and even the prison officers began to ask questions about the power of Jesus Christ. I learned then, that when God showed up like that, witnessing was easy! People were hungry to know all about the Lord and what he could do for them.

During the following weeks we prayed, in faith, for many sick prisoners, and to our great joy, we saw the good hand of God graciously touch the lives of young men, marvellously healing their sicknesses. Prison is no picnic, but I will always cherish those days as precious. I stand today privileged to have seen healings and miracles first-hand. The prison bars kept the prisoners in and the public out, but they couldn't stop the Holy Spirit of God coming down into the prison and bringing the blessing of an open heaven, as the result of a handful of converted prisoners fervently and faithfully praying.

Yes, those prison days were now happy days! God had turned my mourning into dancing, my sorrow into a great joy that knew no limits, and caused me to sing the praises of God constantly. Once my lips only swore, cursed and blasphemed, but now that I was a new person, they blessed God and proclaimed his praise.

Red Band

One day Philip, the chaplain, asked me if I would like to be his chapel orderly. The job was one of three trusted positions in the prison. Those trusted three were called 'Red Bands' because of the red material band they had to wear on their left arm. A Red Band was allowed access to almost every part of the prison, and the job, apart from the kitchens, was considered the best. The salary wasn't bad, but it was a set rate: there could be no overtime like the butcher's job which was the highest-paid job Aylesbury YCC offered. The chaplain's orderly had to clean the chapel everyday and assist the chaplain before, during and after church services. On top of that, the orderly had to clean the chief officers' corridor daily, which was the area I was cleaning one day when I saw the two fire engines come screaming through the two open gates of the prison.

Philip advised me that because I still had more than a year of my sentence to serve, the Governor might reject my application on the grounds that it was a security risk, with the temptation to escape. However, he asked me to think about it overnight, as he would come and see how I felt about it the next day. Although I had grown to love the butcher's job in the kitchen and had a good rapport with the men and officers alike, I sensed that God was in all this, and that meant that it was alright. After praying about the job change, I experienced God's peace in my heart as I went to sleep that evening.

The next day, in spite of Philip's warning of not getting too hopeful, I just knew that the chaplain's orderly job was mine. Sure enough, a week later, I swapped my kitchen whites for the coveted red band. Once again, things changed, and God began to bless me in my new job. I couldn't help but notice how God had so wonderfully prospered me in the prison. My story was in many ways becoming like that of a young man in the Bible called Joseph, who although a captive in an Egyptian prison was noticed by the chief jailer and promoted. *'The chief jailer had no more worries after that, because*

*Joseph took care of everything. The Lord was with him, making
everything run smoothly and successfully.'*[56]

That was my experience, too. I had a bad past, but
because God was with me, the present was getting better
and more glorious day by day.

The Gideon Bibles Collecting Dust

One day, while I was cleaning things up and dusting off
religious statues in the chapel storeroom, I came across a
large box, which was sealed but had 'Gideons
International Youth Testaments' written upon it.
Intrigued, I blew the dust off the box and opened it.
Inside was real treasure in the form of two hundred little
red-covered New Testaments. I knew that these Bibles
were in the wrong place – after all, they had been donat-
ed by the Aylesbury branch of the Gideons to be presented to every prisoner.

Realising the incredible potential these little red
Testaments held, I went and asked Philip if I would be
allowed to distribute them. With his blessing, I made
plans to give them out. I put a table in the foyer corridor
leading into the chapel from the main prison wing, and
began to display all two hundred New Testaments. I
prayed as I placed them on the table that needy, hungry
hearts would take one on the following Sunday at the
church service. I knew that it was by reading the scriptures that I had come to the knowledge of the truth that
had set me free. The words of Jesus Christ came to me . . .
'And you will know the truth, and the truth will set you free.'[57]
What God had done for me, he could do for others, and
these Bibles were going to play their part.

That Sunday morning, just over a hundred of the New
Testaments found their way back to the prisoners' cells.

After Sunday lunch, during lock-up period, I had a time of prayer. I thanked God for the Bibles that had been taken, and I asked the Lord to do what only he could do for these desperate men all around me. That afternoon, I had found a verse in the Bible from the book of Isaiah that boosted my faith as I prayed for those men with their New Testaments. *'It is the same with my word. I send it out, and it always produces fruit. It will accomplish all I want it to, and it will prosper everywhere I send it.'*[58]

A Gideon had placed a Bible at Aylesbury prison, probably years before I was sent there. For some years it may have collected dust and been overlooked. Yet, in the eternal purposes and wisdom of God, I found it and read those glorious pages, finding Christ as my Saviour.

A Gideon had placed a Bible at Aylesbury prison

Armed with the knowledge of the power of God's Word, I slowly distributed the rest of the New Testaments. I would go from cell to cell, witnessing to the life-changing power of Jesus. I would tell the men that they could find the incomparable Christ, as I had, if they would try reading the Bible for themselves. The Apostle John was well aware of the power of the Gospel, and so he began to sum up his account of all that Jesus had said and done by saying: *'But these are written so that you may believe that Jesus is the Messiah, the Son of God, and that by believing in him you will have life.'*[59]

I never guessed then, that one day I would become a member of the Gloucester branch of the Gideons International and have the joy of distributing thousands of New Testaments to schoolchildren, patients in hospital and yes, even prisoners at Gloucester prison. Someone

> *The definition of the Gideons is, 'Absent-minded businessmen who leave their Bibles everywhere!'*

once said that the definition of the Gideons is, 'absent-minded businessmen who leave their Bibles everywhere!' To every faithful Gideon I would like to say thank you on behalf of the thousands who have had a life-changing encounter with the living God through the pages of Gideon scriptures.

Out of the Comfort Zone

Mark was a sad case. He was a large lad who had ugly facial features, and was known cruelly as 'The Hunchback'. From the moment I saw him, I knew that I must speak to him about Jesus. Mark was rejected by the other prisoners and often abused by the violent men on the wing. Something was not right inside Mark's head, as he would often cry out insanely and shriek painfully as he cut himself with razor blades during the night-time bang up period.

Mark was only a couple of cells away from me, and when I heard him go berserk in his cell, it tore my heart. I knew the Lord could set him free from the kingdom of darkness that not only held him captive, but was destroying him as well. As I prayed for Mark one night in my cell, great tears of compassion flowed down my cheeks as I sought God's help on his behalf. Suddenly, whilst I was praying, the Lord spoke to me through the scriptures about the demon-possessed man living in the land of the Gerasenes, whom Jesus had gloriously set free from a thousand evil spirits.[60]

The Holy Spirit gave me what I would later recognise as the gift of discerning of spirits.[61] To the officers and others, mark was just a mad man, but I could see, by the help of the Holy Spirit, that he wasn't mad and didn't need tranquillisers and a padded cell, as some had suggested. No, Mark

> *Mark needed a mighty deliverance from evil, and Jesus Christ was the only answer*

needed a mighty deliverance from evil, and Jesus Christ was the only answer.

The demons obeyed the Lord Jesus Christ in the days he was on earth and I knew with a deep conviction that they would have to obey Christ now. Enough was enough. I was tired of seeing Satan torment this lad, and I was going to pray for Mark with a determined mind to see this young man set free, just as Christ had set me free. When I shared this with others, they all warned me to steer clear, as deliverance and exorcism were jobs for the 'professionals'. Rubbish! I thought to myself, as I considered that Jesus was the 'professional' and the Bible clearly stated that '*I can do everything with the help of Christ who gives me the strength I need.*'[62] Armed with the scriptures that told me it could be done, I prayerfully waited for my chance to minister to Mark.

Someone once said, 'Unless you leave the safety of the shore, you will never discover new oceans!' Time and time again over the years, I have looked at the familiar shoreline of my comfort zone. Then I have set sail into the deep, knowing only the magnetic pull, as it were, of the Holy Spirit drawing me into new oceans and seas of blessings in God. Faith should be vibrant, living and ever-increasing. Through the circumstances of life, God is constantly stretching the faith of those who hunger for more of him.

Some time after the Lord revealed the true problem of demons wreaking havoc in Mark's life, my opportunity came. Because the prison officers didn't know how to handle Mark properly, he was admitted to the prison hospital, which used to be the condemned cells adjoining the execution cell towards the front of the prison. The hospital wing was directly below the chapel, and was accessible from it via a staircase and barred gate.

Mark was admitted to the hospital for observation because he was considered a suicide risk, and the officers were taking no chances with him. As I was cleaning the chapel one morning, I heard a voice calling me through the gate that led through the vestry into the hospital wing staircase. I put down my mop and entered the vestry. There was Mark, standing at the gate, asking for me. I remember looking at this large young man and realising that if I got this wrong, I could get hurt. All the things the others had warned me about flashed through my mind, but I put those fears to one side and concentrated on speaking calmly, but positively, to Mark.

As we talked Mark began to shake all over and his eyes darted nervously, avoiding mine. He then began to cry like a small child, telling me, through his sobs, that he didn't want to be like he was, but something inside made him cut himself and scream out animal noises. I spoke gently of Jesus' love and retold, in my own words, the account of Jesus setting the demon-possessed man free. As Mark listened, his body seemed to shake more violently, and although I was feeling uncomfortable myself now at this manifestation of evil racking his body, I continued to speak on the triumph of the Cross and the wonder-working power of Jesus' blood to cleanse us from all sin. When I felt I had said all I could, I asked mark if he would like to turn from his sins and accept Jesus as his saviour. Suddenly, he smashed his head into the barred gate and screamed, 'yes'. By now, I was feeling a sense of fear, but, taking the bull by the horns, I stretched out my hands through the bars of the gate and grabbed Mark's head. With an anger at Satan and also the authority that I had in Jesus Christ, I prayed over Mark saying, 'Satan I bind your power over Mark right now and command you to leave his body this instant, in the name of Jesus Christ of Nazareth!' Mark's body seemed to thrash about and then, slowly he collapsed to the floor by the barred gate, sobbing.

When he finally looked up at me, his face was different: tear-stained, yes, but definitely changed. The darting shiny eyes that gave away the presence of the evil spirits were now shining with the light of Christ, and his whole body was at peace. We then prayed together and Mark followed me as I led him in a simple prayer of repentance. When Mark had finished praying, I hugged him as best I could through the bars. Yet again, I had seen another triumph of God's amazing grace: a nobody, written off by society, had become somebody – a child of God and an heir of his grace.

That day I learned yet more vital lessons as I grew in my relationship with the Lord. I had authority over demons in Jesus' name, and although things looked scary, I was perfectly safe as I did things God's way and trusted completely in him.

Since then, I have seen many others, like Mark, wonderfully set free through the powerful name of Jesus Christ. Once, years later, I was called to go and speak in Swindon to some young adults who had been dabbling with the occult. I was going into a situation on my own at that time and felt the intimidation of satanic fear trying to oppress me. As I walked through Newent, on my way home, the Spirit of God brought a precious truth to my mind – one that the Apostle Paul had written to the saints at Philippi about hundreds of years earlier. *'Because of this, God raised him up to the heights of heaven and gave him a name that is above every other name, so that at the name of Jesus every knee will bow, in heaven and on earth and under the earth, and every tongue will confess that Jesus Christ is Lord, to the glory of God the Father.'*[63]

The phrase *'God gave him a name'* kept coming to me, and as I walked home along the pavement running to the front of my house the Lord said to me, *'I have given you Jesus' name!'* I knew then that I had nothing to worry about, even in the face of obvious satanic goings-on, because in Jesus' name every knee must bow. As I drove to Swindon that night I had a new confidence, not in anything I could do, but rather in the authority I had over every demon I would come against, in the all-powerful name of Jesus Christ. I have seen demons resist being exorcised, but sooner or later they have all given up and vacated the person being prayed for, as they cannot match the power of prayer in Jesus' name.

There has been much written on deliverance ministry, some good, some bad, but, at the end of the day, the ministry God gave me at that time was effective in its pure simplicity and utter dependence on Jesus Christ's power to set the captives free. I had no knowledge of counselling skills or any academic training to give people professional therapy, but, I knew I had something precious in Jesus Christ that made me seriously rich, and that treasure is for sharing with others.

Protection

While at Aylesbury, I also learned a vital lesson of trusting in God's protection. The lesson served me well because, later on in my Christian life, I have encountered danger while working for the Lord. Although every occasion has had its real possibility of injury to myself, I have been able to be level-headed and have known God's peace, as I have fully trusted in him to protect me. David, before he fought Goliath, the Philistine giant from Gath, [64] had had his experiences of God's protection as he fought against a lion and a bear that had attacked his flocks. David's faith had been strengthened as he thought to himself, 'If God could help me in that situation, he can sure help and protect me right now!' Faith should be ever-increasing and, in my experiences of the past, I can see how my faith has gone through different fires of testing. The Apostle Peter said to the early Christians that the trials prove the genuineness of the faith that we have in God: *'These trials are only to test your faith, to show that it is strong and pure. It is being tested as fire tests and purifies gold – and your faith is far more precious to God than mere gold. So if your faith remains strong after being tried by fiery trials, it will bring you much praise and glory and honour on the day when Jesus Christ is revealed to the whole world.'* [65]

One day, as I was walking through the main prison block, I noticed some black men outside the chapel door on the third floor up. They were waiting for me and, as I approached them, I felt uneasy inside. These young black prisoners were the 'drugs and burn barons' for C wing and had a fearful reputation. They didn't waste their time in pleasantries, but told me I was to be their contraband courier from the main prison block to the high security E and F wings, which were separate and housed all the lifers and category 'A' prisoners. Because of my unique status as a Red Band, I was a trustee and would be their natural choice of prisoner to take forbidden substances around the prison.

I flatly refused, because now that I was a Christian, I disagreed with drugs and was aware I had a testimony of integrity to uphold for Jesus Christ. The three men looked at me in disbelief. Nobody messed around with them, and they were not happy at my refusal. They asked me again, and when I steadfastly refused, the threats came. I was told that if I didn't do as they wanted I would 'accidentally' fall from the top floor of the prison wing to the deck! Although there were suicide nets in place, a fall would be nasty and would probably result in serious injury.

I still said 'no', and so they reminded me of another con who was cut badly on his face weeks earlier. They told me that I would have a face like a jigsaw puzzle if I didn't comply. By now I was terrified but, like Stephen,⁶⁶ the first martyr of the Church, I would have rather died at that point than let Jesus down. Just when I thought I was going to be thrown over the railings, a prison officer began climbing up to our landing and so the men left me alone, warning me that they would be waiting for me as soon as I finished my jobs in the chapel.

As soon as the chapel door was locked behind me, I went straight down to the front of the church and got on my knees before the altar and began to pour out my heart to the Lord. To say I felt afraid of the intimidation and threats of death was an understatement! Feeling a compulsion to read something from the Word of God, I picked up a church pew copy of the Bible and the pages opened it at Psalm 27. Reading those golden words, at that moment, brought to my heart the peace of God that passes all human understanding. *'The Lord is my light and my salvation, so why should I be afraid? The Lord protects me from danger, so why should I tremble? When evil people come to destroy me, when my enemies and foes attack me, they will stumble and fall. Though a mighty army surrounds me, my heart will know no fear. Even if they attack me, I remain confident. The one thing I ask of the Lord – the thing I seek most – is to live in the house of the Lord all the days of my life, delighting in the Lord's perfections and meditating in his Temple. For he will conceal me there when troubles come; he will hide me in his sanctuary. He will place me out of reach on a high rock. Then I will hold my head high, above my enemies who surround me. At his Tabernacle I will offer sacrifices with shouts of joy, singing and praising the Lord with music.'*[67]

The Lord began to minister to my fearful heart through this beautiful psalm of David. I knew that David had had his fair share of troubles and I guessed that if God brought David through, he could also bring me through safely in one piece. I read the psalm a few times and then got on with my duties of cleaning the prison chapel. When it was time to leave, I rang the bell, which indicated to the prison officers that somebody needed to be let out of the chapel. When the door opened, the black men had gone, and I was able to walk back to my cellblock without any more intimidation.

Over the years, I have had people attack me as I have proclaimed the Gospel and sought to help people involved in the kingdom of darkness. Once, a man pulled a knife on me, and although it appeared that he was going to plunge it into my chest, he couldn't. Knowing that the Lord's protection brings peace, I was able to quietly say, 'I command you to drop that knife in Jesus Christ's name.' The young man instantly dropped the weapon and I was able to minister to him.

I command you to drop that knife in Jesus Christ's name

Another time, after I had been freed from Aylesbury, I visited a man in Maidstone prison. As I walked up the crowded main street of the town centre – a stranger among a throng of hundreds – the crowd parted and suddenly a demon-possessed man, yelling and shrieking out blasphemous obscenities, leapt at me as if to knock me down and fight with me. There was no time to pray, but as the violent attacker flew through the air in my direction, he bounced off what could only be described as an invisible shield. Years beforehand, I would have scoffed at such stories, but now I have the benefit of knowing what the Bible says. *'For the angel of the Lord guards all who fear him, and he rescues them.'*[68]

Many years have passed since God marvellously filled me with the Holy Spirit that night at Aylesbury. Living in the power of the Spirit is what God wants for every one of us. I have found, over the years, that as I have obeyed the Lord's word, signs and wonders have frequently taken place: from wonderful healings, to protection from evil and abundant provision of daily needs. I know now though, as I reflect over all that God has done in and through me, that the greatest sign and wonder is when a life is changed through the power of Jesus Christ.

The Gospel of Mark ends with 'the great commission'. The great heart cry of Christ to his followers is to go into the entire world, throughout successive generations, and proclaim the 'Good News' to every man, woman, boy and girl. When people hear the message of truth and decide to believe in Jesus Christ as their Saviour, they are immediately rescued out of the kingdom of darkness and transported into the kingdom of light. People who were like captives awaiting the death sentence on death row are suddenly set free, the broken-hearted are healed, and the blind receive their sight.

The greatest of the signs and wonders are not miracles and stories of healings that generate all sorts of debates from sceptics, but rather the simplicity and wonder of the 'New Birth'. Every time I preach today, I look over a congregation with immense needs and, as I proclaim the glorious message of Jesus Christ, I ask God for the confirming signs and wonders that accompanied the faithful preaching of the Early Church. Today, I preach with a deep passion and a heart that is desperate to see souls getting marvellously saved, because I passionately believe that when someone is 'Born Again' it is the greatest sign and wonder. A miracle of new life has taken

> *I assure you, unless you are born again, you can never see the Kingdom of God*

place! Once, when a truth-seeking religious leader named Nicodemus questioned Jesus about his miracles, Jesus replied, *'I assure you, unless you are born again, you can never see the Kingdom of God.'*[69]

The truth is this: unless you are born again you will never experience new life and have an assurance for the future.

11

A BRIGHT NEW WORLD

As my prison sentence came to an end, I had to find somewhere to live. At first, this seemed a problem, yet I was convinced that God would lead me and take care of me. I talked to one of the prison chaplains about this, and he laughed at me saying that God just didn't do things like giving people divine direction any more! Undeterred, I went back to my cell and prayed that somehow God would show me what to do. As I prayed, peace came over me and I knew that all would be well, after all, my Bible says, *'And we know that God causes everything to work together for the good of those who love God and are called according to his purpose for them.'* [70]

The Lord gave me two wonderful promises from his Word that blessed me then and still bless me today. I believe passionately that the eternal God of the Universe, who sustains everything by the power of his Word, speaks to his people clearly, personally and daily, guiding us into his perfect will for our lives and directing our footsteps in the path he has planned for us to walk in. The Lord says, *'I will guide you along the best pathway for your life. I will advise you and watch over you.'* [71] And also *'Trust in the Lord with all your heart; do not depend on your own understanding. Seek his will in all you do, and he will direct your paths.'* [72]

I dared to believe that God would show me the way forward. Don Moen, a songwriter, inspired by the fact that God delivered his people from the tyranny of Egypt and then miraculously opened up the Red Sea for them wrote . . .

> God will make a way
> Where there seems to be no way,
> He works in ways we cannot see,
> He will make a way for me.
> He will be my guide, hold me closely to his side,
> With love and strength for each new day,
> He will make a way, he will make a way.[73]

Yes it's true, God can make a way where there seems to be no way. I knew that I didn't have to worry about anything, as God had it all in hand. And when it's all in his hand, that makes all the difference.

God can make a way where there seems to be no way

Later that week, I was told I had a visit from Margaret. As I sat down at the table and talked with her, I noticed some people who I had never seen before, smile at me from across the visiting room. They were sitting and talking with Kris. When Margaret went to fetch us a cup of tea, I got up and walked over to their table to say hello. The owners of the smiling faces were introduced as David and Dinah from 'Victory Outreach', based in Gloucester. Victory Outreach is a Christian ministry reaching out to prisoners with the Gospel of Jesus Christ. David and Dinah had a large home in Gloucester where they had other men, from similar backgrounds to mine, living together as a family. Although they had never met me before, we instantly warmed to each other. Kris had told them all about my imminent release from prison and because of that, David and Dinah kindly offered me a place at their Gloucester home.

I knew in my heart right then and there that this was all part of God's care and guidance for me, providing for me a home on my release from prison. The peace of God in my heart confirmed to me that going to Victory Outreach in Gloucester was right. That very night, I wrote to David and Dinah, confirming that I would love to join them in Gloucester as soon as I was released from serving my prison sentence at Aylesbury.

This was the first of many wonderful ways that God took care of the way I was to go. Over the years, I have met people who seem to make God's will very complicated, not only for themselves, but for everyone else! I simply take the Bible to be God's Word for man. As I read the Bible pages daily, the will of God is clearly given to me. The general will of God can be found clearly in many things such as: it's right to go to church; it's right to bring finance as an offering to God; it's right to show practical love; it's right to forgive people; it's right to sing God's praises. The list, which is crystal clear, goes on, guiding us in every aspect of human life.

Even when the path seems to come to a fork and I am not sure which way to go, God says to me, 'Richard, don't use all your intellect, this is an opportunity to grow in faith and trust me. Before you do anything else, talk to me; through prayer and sincere heart-searching, commit it all to me. If you do that, really believing, I will honour your faith and clearly show you the way forward.' To this very day, God has never let me down. After all, didn't Jesus the Good Shepherd say,' *My sheep recognise my voice; I know them, and they follow me.*' [74]

Home Leave

The prison policy, during my days as a convict, was to allow men reaching the end of their sentences a chance to go home for a couple of days on what was called 'Home Leave'. The idea was to help the men make domestic arrangements for their release day. Some prisoners abused the system and failed to come back to the prison on time or, if they did turn up, they would be drunk. Others were arrested for committing another crime!

The prison and the probation service agreed to my application asking for home leave, and allowed me two days at Victory Outreach, Gloucester, under the supervision of David and Dinah. I can remember the mixed emotions of joy and a sense of apprehension, at the prospect of facing something new all over again. The banging doors and the sound of jingling keys turning locks has a strange way of institutionalising you, and although the prison wouldn't be my first choice of residence, it did offer a degree of security in the strictness of its penal regime.

My home leave was scheduled midweek, from Tuesday morning to Thursday morning. Not long, but long enough to breathe the fresh air of freedom. As I was escorted to the gatehouse, I was excited because Margaret had kindly offered to take me to Gloucester, and she had promised to come and collect me. When I had signed the obligatory official release forms, Margaret was allowed into the gatehouse to take me on my journey. Once we were outside the gate, we hugged each other and rejoiced at all that God had done for me. Margaret first took me to her own home and made me welcome. I had a nice surprise waiting for me there. Katherine and Carol, Margaret's two daughters, were waiting to greet me. In fact, they were going that

very day to a Christian camp in Gloucestershire and so
would be joining us for most of our journey.

What a journey that was. The rain was absolutely pour-
ing down, talk about, 'Dr Foster went to Gloucester in a
shower of rain!' To make things
more interesting, Katherine was
learning to drive and she was
behind the wheel. The poor visi-
bility and the inefficiency of the
windscreen wipers didn't deter
her from putting her foot down!
The spray of those large lorries she
kept getting close to drenched the
car, and I found myself quietly
repeating, *'The Lord is my Shepherd . . . Even when I walk
through the dark valley of death . . .'*[75]

> *The poor visibility
> and the inefficiency
> of the windscreen
> wipers didn't deter
> her from putting
> her foot down!*

Thankfully, our silent fervent prayers marvellously
helped Katherine's driving skills, and we made it to the
camp in record time. Once Margaret had said goodbye to
the girls we started out once again towards Gloucester. As
we approached the city, the sun's rays burst down from
the heavens like a huge spotlight upon the magnificent
tower of Gloucester Cathedral. Looking at the splendid
view through the car windscreen, I felt God whisper to
my heart, 'I am with you, don't be afraid.'

Margaret had never been to the cathedral before, and
so asked me if I would like to walk around the 900-year-
old building. Walking around the cathedral, we found a
little side chapel and stopped long enough to pray for
each other. I felt a twinge of sadness creep upon me at
that point, as I knew my contact with Margaret would
soon come to an end. Margaret and John would have
gladly sacrificed the comfort of their home and made
space for one more. They had talked about it and were

only too glad to help me and offer me a home. I was sad, because I would have dearly liked that to have happened. I would have loved to have settled at Aylesbury with them, to be part of their church, which I had heard so much about. To have been a part of their daily lives would have been heaven for me, but it wasn't to be so.

I didn't know at that point what God had for me at Gloucester, but I knew, without any shadow of doubt, that this great cathedral city of more than a hundred thousand people was where I had to be at that time.

Margaret's car pulled up outside All Saints vicarage, the home of Victory Outreach. The door was opened, and before we knew it, we were sitting in the lounge with a cup of tea. The conversation seemed to be hard-going. I think Margaret was feeling the strain by now, and she was probably relieved to start back for Aylesbury.

Robinswood Pentecostal Church

David and Dinah took the lads at Victory Outreach to the local Assemblies of God Pentecostal Church on Robinswood Hill, overlooking Gloucester. Robinswood Pentecostal Church had a Bible study on Wednesday nights, so I was asked if I would like to go. This was a whole new experience for me, as I had never been to a Pentecostal church before, and I didn't really know what to expect. Walking into the building, I was taken aback by the

Pointing to the banjo-playing singer on the platform I whispered, 'Is he the warm-up man?' To my shock she answered, 'No, he's the pastor!'

sheer simplicity of it all: just a plain hall with a raised platform at one end, no stained glass, no crosses on the wall, no choir in robes. I couldn't see any minister either. I sat down with the others from Victory Outreach on the back row and observed the proceedings. The meeting started with a lady beginning to sing short songs which I later identified as 'choruses'. After a while, a slender looking man wearing a smart suit came from a side door into the main hall and walked onto the platform. All eyes seemed to be on this man with a Liverpudlian accent, and to my amusement, he began to play a little banjo instrument. The man got the ladies to sing first, and then he got the men to sing and finally everyone to sing together. All this went on for some time. Eventually, I became concerned about the minister, after all the service had begun and he should have been there. Leaning over to Dinah and pointing to the banjo-playing singer on the platform I whispered, 'Is he the warm-up man?' To my shock she answered, 'No, he's the pastor!'[76]

The home leave soon came to an end, and David and Dinah got me back to Aylesbury on time. As I waved goodbye to them outside the gate, I gritted my teeth and knocked on the little door by the large gates. Moments later, I was back inside prison, and an hour later back in my little cell. It was tough, but I knew that God was with me and I would soon be released and going to Gloucester to fulfil my destiny in God.

The days flew by, and before I knew it I was seeing the prison Governor for the last time. I was taken to the induction wing and given some clothes and a small amount of money called a 'discharge grant'. Margaret met me again at the prison gates and drove me halfway to Gloucester, stopping at Burford, where we met David and Dinah, who took me the rest of the way to my new home in Gloucester.

Gloucester

Once at Gloucester with David and Dinah, I joined Robinswood Pentecostal Church. I loved this church, and although the people knew all about my wretched past, they accepted me as a brother and welcomed me whole-heartedly into the church family. People would ask me back to their homes for supper after the Sunday evening meeting and, as I ate sandwiches and cakes with my new church family, I would spend many joyful hours talking about the goodness of God. Before long, Pastor Garner had my name on his baptismal list. He was preaching one Sunday that Jesus had commanded his followers to be baptised. I knew that Pastor Garner was right, for I had searched the scriptures for myself and realised that Jesus said, '*If you love me, obey my commandments.*'[77]

Although I was certainly saved and also filled with the Holy Spirit, I knew that it was right to submit to Jesus' command and be baptised. This was my chance to publicly nail my colours to the mast and take my place at the Cross of Jesus Christ. Pastor Garner explained that baptism was like a funeral service. He said that the old me, all that longed and lusted after sin, was dead, and so needed to be buried symbolically in the baptismal waters. The Apostle Paul put it this way when he wrote about baptism, '*For you were buried with Christ when you were baptised. And with him you were raised to a new life because you trusted the mighty power of God, who raised Christ from the dead.*'[78]

When the baptismal night came around, I felt very nervous, not because of the slender frame of Pastor Garner and his dubious ability to bring me up out of the water, but because of the great crowd of people that had gathered to watch the event. Mike Anders, one of the church officers had rigged up a video camera, complete with a great big halogen spotlight, which made all those being baptised feel even more nervous. The service started with worship songs and somebody gave a short sermon. Then, when Pastor Garner and Ernie Miles, the church treasurer were ready, they entered the baptismal pool and called out our names, one by one. I was the third person to be called. I rose, climbed the steps onto the platform at the front of the church and then, half-blinded by the halogen spotlight, testified to my salvation. I explained that I was being baptised because I loved Jesus and wanted to obey him by following him through the waters of baptism.

It was all over so quickly. All those anxious moments were suddenly gone: I was baptised, and as I rose out of the water, it was with a note of triumph. I had taken another step in following my Lord. Just as the heavens opened as Jesus Christ was baptised by John the Baptist in the river Jordan two thousand years earlier, with the Holy Spirit descending upon Jesus, so the heavens opened for me. God anointed me with the oil of gladness as I climbed out of the pool, totally soaked, but rejoicing in the Lord. Later, when we had all dried off, Pastor Garner presented us each with a baptism certificate, which I have to this day.

> *I was baptised, and as I rose out of the water, it was with a note of triumph*

The Word of the Lord

Those early days in Gloucester were very busy for me, as I was reaching out to those behind bars by visiting and also writing letters. I was fulfilled in my prison ministry, but I knew that this was not what God had called me to. I knew about God's general will for my life, as I have already mentioned, but through the hectic schedule of those Victory Outreach days, I sensed God directing my steps in a different direction to that which everyone was trying to tell me. I had to learn then that it was sensible to listen to good counsel, but, as Pastor Garner used to say constantly about God's guidance, 'Jesus said, *"My sheep hear my voice and follow me."* '[79]

Each day I would pray and ask God why I felt unsettled at Victory Outreach. I would read my Bible and listen to what God was saying to me. I knew I had to be patient and that it would be sheer folly to do anything rash. When you are in doubt about the will of God, it's always best to continue with a faithful heart, doing what God last instructed you to do. We are always in a rush, but God isn't, for he knows the end from the beginning and he knows what he will do.

Then, one night as I went to hear a Bible teacher in a school hall in Cheltenham, something amazing happened that would change the course of my life. During the day, the devil had been attacking my thoughts with the accusation that I didn't really love God, and that when I worshipped God it was all a sham. I guess every Christian has come under that sort of attack at some point in their life – that day it was my turn! I felt wretched as I battled against Satan, and, as the day went on, I felt utterly condemned as he told me I was ineffective as a Christian witness and that my life would come to nothing. By the time evening came and we drove to Cheltenham, I pleaded with God to sort out all the mess I seemed to be in, and asked him somehow to speak to me clearly about my future.

> *'It's not over until God says so!'*

The message the preacher brought was a good one: all about the Prophet Jeremiah's servant called Baruch, who was warned not to seek great things for himself. I listened to the message from the preacher, yet I still felt I needed to hear specifically from God. The meeting was almost over and the last hymn was being sung. My heart was sinking, but I encouraged myself with a familiar phrase that Pastor Garner often used, 'It's not over until God says so!' Suddenly the preacher looked at me and asked me to come to the front of the congregation – this had never happened to me before!

Feeling nervous, I walked slowly forward, but once I stood at the front of the hall, I knew that I was on holy ground. God was there and he began to speak directly to me through the mouth of the preacher, who prophesied over me. God began to speak about things in my life that only God, and God alone, could possibly know. The Lord said clearly to me that he knew I lived to worship him, and my praise which flowed from a heart that was in love with him was a joy to his ears. Now, that was a resounding blow to the Devil! To top that, God continued to speak to me through the preacher, telling me that he had called me to the ministry and that he would anoint me with great power to preach the Gospel of Jesus Christ and to serve his people. The prophecy ended with the truth that the more I sought God, the more he would anoint me for my new ministry.

The preacher never once touched me as he prophesied over me – in fact, he stood away from me. He then prayed that God would do for me all that he had promised through the prophecy. The power of God came upon me and I found myself on the floor! This was an incredible experience, as nobody had touched me or pushed me in any way. From time to time, when the glorious presence of God is manifested in a service, people who are touched by the power of God sometimes fall to the floor as the weight of God's glory comes upon them. The acid test to anything like this is: How does the person's life change as a result of the experience? For, if the experience is from God, he will cause fruit to grow from that experience which will glorify his name. When I rose from the floor, I knew that I had met with God and that if I surrendered my entire life to him, exciting things would happen. I knew that God had revealed himself to me for a purpose and I had to keep close to him to discover all that he had in store for me.

After that awesome night with God I, began to witness more. In fact, I would often walk into Gloucester city centre armed with a bundle of gospel tracts, determined not to return home until every one had been given out. I would get up early in the morning, reading and studying my Bible more than before. At that time, God began to use me through spiritual gifts in the local church, with the gift of giving messages in tongues. I was doing all I could to be involved in ministry, and yet nothing seemed to be happening. However, I learned to be faithful in that which God had given me to do.

Two Are Better Than One

God said it wasn't good for Adam, the first man, to be alone,[80] and I realised it wasn't good for me to be alone either. I had not thought much about girls after coming out of prison. After all, I was too busy! But God was going to change all that, as he knew then that I was going to need a companion for life who would stand with me and support me in the ministry days that lay ahead.

Lynne was a young woman at Robinswood Pentecostal Church who had given up her job to come to Victory Outreach to serve God. From the time of our first meeting, I knew that she was the one for me. We would sit in the kitchen talking about the things of God with the other lads, but we found ourselves spending more and more time together. I knew she was a great girl: intelligent, attractive, fun-loving, hard-working, but, even more importantly, a girl who loved Jesus just as much as I did. As I thought about the old chat-up lines I had rehearsed so many times with girlfriends in the past, God spoke to my heart and told me to ask her to marry me!

Knowing that God never makes mistakes, I waited for the right moment. I didn't have the financial resources to wine and dine Lynne so, one day, I managed to get her to come with me to visit a man in Featherstone prison. Waiting to go into the prison, Lynne and I sat outside the gates in the warm sunshine of a summer's day. The moment was right – not romantic by any means – but right, so I got down on one knee and asked Lynne to marry me, and of course, she said, 'Yes!'

I got down on one knee and asked Lynne to marry me, and of course, she said, 'Yes!'

Blessings

Lynne and I realised that it was time to leave Victory Outreach, and although we had no money and nowhere to go, God made a way where there seemed no way. Lynne's mum allowed us to stay at her house. I had a room to myself and Lynne shared a bedroom with her younger sister. It was amazing: at the start of the day I wondered where I would be sleeping, and now at the end of the day, I had my own comfortable room. That night, I put my head on the pillow and praised God for every blessing he had given me: a beautiful and loving girl-friend who would soon be my wife, a new place to live, and the Robinswood Church family. Yes, as I lay there in bed contemplating God's blessing upon my life, once again, I realised that I was seriously rich.

I realised that God's will was for me to get a job and settle into a normal routine until he placed me in the ministry as a preacher. One morning, I read a verse from my Bible that seemed to leap out of the pages at me: '*He who has been stealing must steal no longer, but must work, doing something useful with his own hands, that he may have something to share with those in need.*' [81] It couldn't be any clearer than that! As I have already said, the will of God is simple to find, for the Bible is God's voice speaking clearly to all who want to hear. The problem I had was that although I had heard from God and was going for lots of job interviews, because of my prison record nobody seemed to want me. I knew I had a new life, but I needed somehow to prove it to an employer. I went from interview to interview, and every time I was asked about my past, I truthfully explained that I had been in prison. As soon as I mentioned the word 'prison' the interviewer would make excuses, and I left feeling dis-heartened. Thankfully, Lynne had got a job quickly and so we were able to help with the housekeeping through her earnings. Those days were pretty tough, as I could have so easily lied about my past and probably got away with it. That, however, was no way to behave now that I was a Christian. To have lied would have been sinful, and I didn't want to build my future on deceit, but on truth.

I had that scripture verse still burning in my heart, and so one day I approached Pastor Garner just before the weekly prayer meeting. With eyes filling up, I poured out my heart to him, sharing my feeling of despair, but also telling him of my Bible verse. That night he told the congregation that I wanted to work but was finding it hard because of my criminal record. Those dear folk prayed fervently for me and God heard from heaven. Pastor Garner would often tell us that we should put legs on our prayers. In other words, we must do what we can do, and then trust God to do what only he can do. The very next day I went to a plastic factory in Gloucester and was interviewed. I was absolutely truthful about everything and, to my surprise, the interviewer asked me if I was in any current trouble with the police. When I satisfied him that I wasn't, and didn't intend to be either, he said, 'You can start next week!'

I learned two important lessons through all that: firstly that God will bless those who walk with integrity, and secondly, although I could pray on my own, the breakthrough in that situation came only when the church stood with me in prayer agreement. Jesus spoke about the power of united prayer to his disciples. '*I also tell you this: If two of you agree down here on earth concerning anything you ask, my Father in heaven will do it for you.*'[82]

The Early Church often prayed together and saw the mighty power of God at work. I learned to love those weekly prayer meetings, as I spent hours in God's presence seeking the face of the Lord for the needs of others. The prayer meeting was a place of action, as God responded to the faith of his people, often through the dynamic vocal gifts of the Holy Spirit. I expected things to happen after a prayer meeting at Robinswood. After all, God himself said, *'Call upon me and I will answer you and show you great and wonderful things.'*[83]

As Lynne and I made preparations for our wedding day, we sought God in prayer to meet all our needs. We had no savings of our own and so we were desperate for divine help. As the days drew closer to our wedding date, although I had changed my job already, I was now looking for a more permanent job that would pay a living salary. Lynne and I were totally convinced that if we sought first the kingdom of God and his righteousness, all the other things we needed would be added to us. Three miracles were granted to us in those days before our wedding.

The first miracle was Lynne's job situation. She had been working hard for a roofing company, but it was a long way from home to travel by bike or foot, and the wages were not much for the work she was doing. One night, Lynne pointed out a job with the city council, which was advertised in the local newspaper. The job was a clerical position at the Gloucester crematorium. The position appealed to Lynne, so we prayed together about it and Lynne secured an interview. After the interview, Lynne was sure that the job was right for her: the work was good and so was the salary, with prospects for the future. The only problem was, ninety other people had applied for the job and the crematorium superintendent had made it clear he wasn't really interested in a younger woman, in case she wanted to leave after a short time to start a family. Everything seemed to be stacked against us, but we knew

If God is for us, who can ever be against us?

that night, as we knelt down to pray together about the job, that God was certainly with us. As the scripture says, '*If God is for us, who can ever be against us*?'[84] Not long after, we rejoiced when Lynne was informed the job was hers!

We had seen a miracle with Lynne's job, and now I was praying about my job situation. At that time, I was working very hard as a chef's assistant in a private hospital in Gloucester. The work wasn't pleasant and the pay was very low for the hours I put in. One day, I noticed that a butcher in Gloucester was looking for an experienced shopman and cutter for part-time work. I telephoned the butcher and asked if I could attend for an interview. He agreed to see me after work on the very next Saturday afternoon. I rode up to the shop and went in feeling nervous. The butcher put me at ease and, over a cup of tea, informally interviewed me. I explained that I had a criminal past, and he didn't seem too bothered. So, feeling bold and wanting the job, I made a proposition to him: I would work for him for one week and if he didn't like my performance he could ask me to leave and he wouldn't have to pay me anything. He agreed, and asked me to turn up on the Tuesday morning at 7 a.m. When I later told Lynne about my proposition to the butcher, she thought I was going crazy, but, 'wisdom is justified by her children'!

That first half-day back in the butchers' shop was a joy: the smell of sawdust and the familiar work of that ancient trade made me happy. It was a miracle that I got back into a trade I really enjoyed, but the best was yet to come! By the end of the first shift, the butcher came to me and asked if I had enjoyed myself. When I replied that I had, he made a proposition to me: he told me that he would double what I was earning at the hospital, if I would come and work for him full-time. That afternoon I had great delight in handing in my notice to the hotel service manager of the private hospital.

God was being good to both of us, and how we thanked him for it. That was two miracles, but we needed a third. Being able to live with Lynne's mum was a real help to us, but we knew that we wanted our own home before the wedding. We went house-hunting and then realised that to get a mortgage we would need a deposit, and we didn't have one because saving money for anything but our wedding was impossible, even on our combined incomes. Disappointed, we looked at some flats in Gloucester and found that demoralising, as most of the places we saw were small, dirty and cost far too much for what they were. Lynne told me that she felt God had something better for us, and if we moved into a flat, we would be making a big mistake. I knew deep down that she was right and that God would give us something better if we would be patient and trust him.

We were praying together about the house problem, and knew it was now going to take a miracle to get in on the housing market. The days went by and the wedding loomed closer and closer. We prayed more fervently, and then one day the answer came. A couple at Robinswood Pentecostal Church, who had known Lynne for years, offered to give us a large sum of money as an interest-free loan so that we could put a deposit down on our first house. With the promise of the cash from our friends, the situation was turned around and, within a few weeks, we had our starter home – a two-bedroomed house in Gloucester.

So, on the 19th September 1987, we were married at Robinswood Pentecostal Church, Gloucester. We had put God first in our lives and in our relationship, and now we were enjoying God's richest blessings that are for all those who trust him and yield their lives to him. People stepped in and helped us with the details for our wedding day: Irene Clack, who had known Lynne since she was a girl made a beautiful three tiered cake; Val Perrins made an exquisite dress; and Mike Anders, who filmed my baptism offered to video the occasion. We even had people we didn't know very well personally giving us wonderful wedding gifts. When we surveyed all our gifts the day after we were married and reflected on the events of our big day, how we praised God for every blessing he had showered upon us. God indeed had made us rich! We were starting off our married life together, not just as a young couple in love, but also as a couple who had the presence of God. To date we have had fifteen great years of marriage, and we can testify to God's help every day, through both tough times and good times.

Two of the greatest blessings we have received from God since we were married are our two sons, Joshua and Samuel. Those two boys have been the joy of our hearts – they have given us sleepless nights and grey hairs too! Raising my two sons has taught me so much about our relationship with God. Watching them relate to me and ask me for help with such simplistic trust, has brought me to a greater place of trust in my heavenly father. I sometimes think about how I treat my boys. I want what is best for them, and so when they ask for things that I know will either harm them or do them no good, I say 'No'. This is not because I am an old, mean, tight-fisted Scrooge, but because I want the best for them. Through the simple lessons of parenting, I have come to a greater understanding of what it really means to be a child of God. Both boys have grown to love the Lord, and we take great delight in going to church together as a family to worship God.

Ministry

God was as good as his word to me. In the early 1990s, he clearly told Lynne and me that it was time to start my public ministry. I began training as an Assemblies of God minister and on completion of my probationary period, I was ordained in April 1996. Since those early days of public ministry, Lynne and I have had many exciting adventures serving God together. We have seen countless lives, which were ruined, just like mine, transformed through faith in Jesus Christ. We have also had the joy of seeing many sick people healed through the mighty power of Jesus Christ.

Over the years, God has guided us and marvellously taken care of all our needs. Sadly, there is no room to tell of the miraculous provision of God, as those miracles would literally take a whole new book! One thing I can say though is this: where God guides – he also provides. Many years ago, I learned that God's promises are not to be framed and hung over the mantelpiece, but rather to be obtained by faith. One such promise says, *'But my God shall supply all your need according to his riches in glory by Christ Jesus.'*[85]

God's promises are not to be framed and hung over the mantelpiece, but rather to be obtained by faith

I have not only committed that wonderful promise to my memory, but I also enjoy its incredible reality daily. No wonder I'm seriously rich!

12

YOU TOO CAN BE SERIOUSLY RICH

Some time ago, I was invited to speak at a church in Gloucester. I was preaching on how Jesus Christ had changed my life, making me seriously rich: not in bank notes and gold, but in true riches, such as God's love, joy and peace. As I was bringing my message to a conclusion, a man stood to his feet and began to walk down the aisle toward the pulpit where I was standing. With tears in his eyes, and with a loud voice he kept saying, 'I want what Richard's got!'

I fought back tears myself, as the pastor came forward and put his loving arms around this man and quietly led him to Jesus Christ, through a simple prayer of repentance and faith.

Maybe as you have read this book there is a voice calling out from the emptiness of your heart saying, 'I want what Richard's got.' The good news is that you can possess what I have, for you, too, can know Jesus Christ as your personal Saviour. That's why I quoted the words of the song at the beginning of the book . . .

It is no secret what God can do,
What he's done for others, he can do for you!

No one is beyond God's love. The Bible clearly says, '*For God so loved the world . . .* ' meaning that if you're reading this book, on this beautiful planet we call 'earth', then God's love is extended to you. God wants to make you seriously rich. He wants to fill your whole life with true treasure that will satisfy your heart and make you the happiest person on earth.

There is no magic formula to becoming the person God longs for you to be. There is no ritualistic service to make you the brand new person for whom Jesus died. In the front of our church we have some provoking words, stuck onto the plain brick wall in large clear letters: 'ONLY BELIEVE'. The Gospel is simple so that every one of us can grasp it and enjoy its marvellous truth. Over the weeks and years, I have seen countless people turn their lives over to Jesus Christ: from those who have all that the world offers, to those who literally have nothing. They come to a life-changing faith in

Jesus is not intimidated by how bad your past is, as his power can remove your guilt and bring you into a marvellous future

Christ. I have heard many stories just like mine, and many far worse. Jesus is not intimidated by how bad your past is, as his power can remove your guilt and bring you into a marvellous future.

Jesus Christ is the mighty Son of God who can transform your life into something beautiful, just as he did mine. He is all powerful and if you come to him with simple faith, trusting in his word as I did, he will turn your . . . Guilty to Not Guilty . . . Death to Life . . . Darkness to Light . . . Hatred to Love . . . Weakness to Power . . . Bondage to Freedom . . . Tribulation to Triumph . . . Grief to Joy . . . Gloom to Glory . . . Defeat to

Victory . . . Failure to Success . . . Fear to Faith . . . I Can't to I Can!

Yes, when you believe in Jesus Christ and come to him, not only can he make you seriously rich, he also will seriously change your whole life. That's why Jesus talked about being 'Born Again'. He literally gives you the incredible experience of starting a completely new life.

We often sing a little song in our church that helps express the wonderful change that Jesus has brought to those who have come to him by faith . . .

> Something beautiful, something good,
> All my confusion he understood.
> All I had to offer him, was brokenness and strife,
> But he made something beautiful out of my life. [86]

If you truly want to be seriously rich, by enjoying the abundant, exciting life that only Jesus Christ can offer, you need to do two vital things. First, you must repent. That means turning away from the things you are doing wrong and turn to God. Jesus was absolutely clear about repentance: '*At last the time has come!*' he announced. '*The Kingdom of God is near! Turn from your sins and believe this Good News!*'[87]

Jesus was telling the people to repent, to acknowledge their sins, to change their minds and the whole way they lived their lives. We have been running away from God, living life our own way, but repentance means we stop running away from God and do a U-turn so that, in fact, we are now running to God.

Many people get confused over the issue of sin. Because they have never committed crimes such as I had done, they feel they are righteous and probably should have no problem with an entrance one day into heaven. Sin is more than somebody breaking the law of the land: it's man's choice to reject God and defiantly stand in rebellion against him and all he desires for our lives. People everywhere are breaking the Ten Commandments all the time! God's moral codes for happy and holy living are flouted and trodden underfoot by the masses who consider that they are right with God because of their own DIY set of moral codes and occasional church attendance. In fact, the attitude of self-righteousness is far more deadly than sins committed openly. That's why the Bible says, *'The heart is deceitful above all things and desperately wicked.'* [88]

Self-righteousness is certainly deceiving many people. God sees and knows the thoughts, intents and actions of every heart and says, *'For all have sinned; all fall short of God's glorious standard.'*[89]

There is no getting away from the truth, as painful as it seems to many 'good' people. We must accept the fact that we are all sinful because of free choice. Every one of us, no matter how rich or famous, needs a Saviour to remove our sins and replace them with his righteousness to make us acceptable to the God who created the universe. Gerrit Gustafson, a modern hymn-writer put it like this . . .

Only by grace can we enter, only by grace can we stand;
Not by our human endeavour, but by the blood of the lamb
Into your presence you call, you call us to come.
Into your presence you draw us and now by your grace we come.

Lord, if you mark our transgression, who would stand?

Lord, if you mark our transgressions, who would stand?
Thanks to your grace we are cleansed by the blood of the Lamb[90]

Unlike many who resist the convicting presence of
God's Holy Spirit, I was in no doubt that I was a sinner
and needed to be saved. Repentance means that we
must also confess our sins to God. To confess our sins is
more than just admitting them and saying a quick
'sorry', like a child wanting to appease an angry parent.
Confession actually means to see our sins through the
eyes of God: in other words, to feel the way God does
about all we do wrong. Now, that is more than a quick
'sorry.' I saw that my sins were so defiling and depraved
that they had angered God and caused him to place the
death sentence upon me, eternal hell.

When I saw the Cross as God's greatest demonstration
of love ever manifested in all eternity, I loathed my sins
that placed Christ through such agony. I hated my sins,
which brought Jesus to this world, to be despised and
rejected, to be arrested, to be mocked, to be whipped until
the flesh hung off his back. To have a crown of cruel thorns
thrust upon his brow and then to be made to carry his own
cross through the maddened crowd; the blood from his
wounds dripping along the way, leaving a trail to be cal-
lously trampled underfoot by shouting, abusive people
who followed to see the final spectacle as a naked man was
nailed to a cross and lifted up to die in excruciating pain.

The second vital thing we must do is to believe in and
receive, Jesus Christ as our Saviour. To do that, we must
ask him into our hearts to take up residence: to sit upon
the throne of our lives, to be our Lord and to make the
changes that are needed deep within us. Why not make
the following prayer your prayer, and be amazed at what
God will do for you.

Lord Jesus Christ

I am sorry for the things I have done wrong in my life, please for give me.

(Take a few moments to ask God's forgiveness for anything in particular that may be on your conscience right now.)

I now turn from everything that I know is wrong.

Thank you for dying for me on the cross so that I could be forgiven and set free, from my sins.

Thank you for the offer of forgiveness and the gift of everlasting life, which I now receive.

Please come into my life and be my Lord and Saviour.

Amen

God promises to hear all those who call to him through the name of his Son Jesus Christ. If you sincerely prayed that prayer and really meant it, then you are now saved, and seriously rich. As the Bible says, '*For if you confess with your mouth that Jesus is Lord and believe in your heart that God raised him from the dead, you will be saved.*'[91]

This book is now almost finished, and it's time for me to lay down my pen. In closing, however, I can't help wondering to myself, what you will do next? If you have read about what Jesus Christ has done for me and have a little faith because of my story, then you are like the man who walked through the field and found treasure. You see, Jesus Christ is the greatest discovery that anyone can ever make. The question is, what will you do with the discovery? Will you walk away and forget about it? To do so, would mean that you have passed up the world's greatest treasure: riches that will

What will you do next?

certainly bless your life beyond your wildest dreams. Or, will you be like the man that Jesus spoke of, who sold everything he had so that he could go and buy the field and possess the discovered treasure?[92]

I will have to leave that decision with you. As for me, I am going to continue to enjoy my discovery of new life in Jesus Christ – treasure indeed that has made me seriously rich.

WHAT NEXT?

Maybe you have read my story and decided to trust Jesus Christ as your Saviour. If you prayed the simple prayer that I included in Chapter 12, you will have asked Jesus Christ into your life. Congratulations, you are now saved! Now that you are 'born again' through the power of God, all things will become new, life will never be the same again, your poverty has been turned to God's prosperity. In fact, you are seriously rich because . . .

1. Jesus Christ Has Come Into Your Life

Its incredible, God, who created the vastness and splendour of the universe, can live anywhere he wants to – and he chose your heart! Because you have invited God into your life to take up residence and to reign in your heart, he will prove to you day by day his great faithfulness. God says . . . *'I will never fail you. I will never forsake you.'*[93]

2. You Have Been Completely Forgiven

That's right! Everything you have ever done wrong is forgiven and forgotten by God. The Bible says . . . *'He cancelled the record that contained the charges against us. He took it and destroyed it by nailing it to Christ's cross.'*[94]

3. You Will Start To Experience 'Life' As God Intended

Up to now, you have been separated from God because of your sins. Sin separates us from God and separation from God means it's impossible to enjoy life to the full. As my friend once said . . . 'You can have a full life, but without Jesus, it's not life to the full!' Jesus said . . . *'My purpose is to give life in all its fullness!'*[95]

Not long after becoming a Christian I started singing a little song that summed up my wonderful life-changing experience in Jesus Christ:

> Jesus makes the difference in me
> Jesus makes the difference in me
> Once my heart was bound by sin
> But now praise God its free
> For Jesus makes the difference in me! [96]

If you have accepted Jesus Christ as your Lord and Saviour you can be absolutely sure that you now have new life because the Bible says . . . *'And this is what God has testified: he has given us eternal life, and this life is in his Son. So whoever has God's Son has life; whoever does not have his Son does not have life. I write this to you who believe in the Son of God, so that you may know you have eternal life.'*[97]

When you experience new life in Jesus it's like being 'Born Again' you are now like a 'baby' spiritually – but don't worry God wants you to grow! God has provided you with the means for strong healthy Christian growth, so that you can live for his glory and know what it is to be victorious over the power of sin.

Steps For Christian Growth

Get to know God by reading the Bible every day.

The Bible says . . . *'All Scripture is inspired by God and is useful to teach us what is true and to make us realize what is wrong in our lives. It straightens us out and teaches us to do what is right. It is God's way of preparing us in every way, fully equipped for every good thing God wants us to do. '*[98]

Relate to God by praying to him every day.

The Bible says . . . *'Don't worry about anything; instead, pray about everything. Tell God what you need, and thank him for all he has done.'*[99]

Obey God in the things you know you should every day.

The Bible says . . . *'And now, just as you accepted Christ Jesus as your Lord, you must continue to live in obedience to him.'*[100]

Walk in the power of God's Holy Spirit every day.

The Bible says . . . *'When I think of the wisdom and scope of God's plan, I fall to my knees and pray to the Father, the Creator of everything in heaven and on earth. I pray that from his glorious, unlimited resources he will give you mighty inner strength through his Holy Spirit.'*[101]

Tell other people about what Jesus has done for you as much as you can.

Jesus said . . . *'If anyone acknowledges me publicly here on earth, I will openly acknowledge that person before my Father in heaven.'*[102]

Have fellowship with other Christians by attending a good evangelical church.

The Bible says . . . *'And all the believers met together constantly and shared everything they had. They sold their possessions and shared the proceeds with those in need. They worshiped together at the Temple each day, met in homes for the Lord's Supper, and shared their meals with great joy and generosity.'*[103]

The Bible says . . . *'And let us not neglect our meeting together, as some people do, but encourage and warn each other, especially now that the day of his coming back again is drawing near.'*[104]

If you would like to talk to someone about the Bible and its message of life through Jesus Christ, why not contact your local branch of The Gideons. You can find their local contact number in the Telephone directory under 'The Gideons International'.

REFERENCES

1. 2 Corinthians 8:9. Scripture taken from the THE MES-SAGE. Copyright © by Eugene H. Peterson, 1993, 1994, 1995, 1996. Used by permission of NavPress Publishing Group.

2. 'It is No Secret' by Stuart Hamblen © 1950 Hamblen Music Co. California.

3. 2 Corinthians 5:17

4. Jo Izatt

5. Jeremiah 17:9

6. Ephesians 3:20

7. John 3:16

8. John 15:13. Scripture taken from KING JAMES VERSION. Copyright © 1970, 2001 by Thomas Nelon Inc. Used by permission.

9. 1 John 1:5–9

10. Matthew 6:5–7. Scripture taken from the THE MESSAGE. Copyright © 1993,1994, 1995, 1996. Used by permission of NavPress Publishing Group.

11. Revelation 20:11–15

12. Revelation 3:20

13. Romans 10:9–10

14. Mark 2:5

15. Psalm 103:8–12

16. Proverbs 10:22
17. Matthew 13:44
18. 2 Corinthians 8:9
19. Ephesians 1:5
20. John 10:28–30
21. John 14:16–17
22. 2 Peter 1:20–21
23. 2 Timothy 3:15–17
24. Matthew 4:4. Scripture taken from the HOLY BIBLE, NEW INTERNATIONAL VERSION. Copyright © 1973, 1978, 1984 by International Bible society. Used by permission of Hodder & Stoughon, a member of Hodder Headline Ltd. All rights reserved.
25. Psalm 1:1–3
26. Romans 8:29
27. Jeremiah 33:3
28. Leonard Ravenhill
29. Hebrews 10:19–20
30. *Illustrations Unlimited* edited by James S. Hewett © 1988. Used by permission of Tyndale House Publisers, Inc. All rights reserved.
31. Hebrews 10:25
32. Acts 18:9–10
33. Matthew 18:20
34. Matthew 5:11–12
35. Matthew 5:38–39
36. Ephesians 6:10–12
37. Psalm 68:6
38. Psalm 51:1–2
39. Psalm 51:15–17
40. Acts 2:1–4; Acts 10: 44–46; Acts 19:1–7; 1 Corinthians 12:7–11
41. 1 Corinthians 14:4
42. Romans 8:26
43. 1 Corinthians 14:1

44. Matthew 3:11
45. Acts 2
46. Acts 1:8
47. Acts 2:39
48. John 7:37–39
49. Matthew 3:11
50. Acts 19:2
51. Ephesians 5:18–20
52. Mark 16:15–20
53. Hebrews 13:8
54. Mark 9:22–23
55. 'Majesty, Worship his Majesty' by Jack W Hayford. Copyright © Rocksmith Music/Leosong Copyright services 1976.
56. Genesis 39:23
57. John 8:32
58. Isaiah 55:11
59. John 20:31
60. Luke 8:26–39
61. 1 Corinthians 12:10
62. Philippians 4:13
63. Philippians 2:9–11
64. 1 Samuel 17
65. 1 Peter 1:7
66. Acts 7
67. Psalm 27:1–6
68. Psalm 34:7
69. John 3:3
70. Romans 8:28
71. Psalm 32:8
72. Proverbs 3:5–6
73. 'God will make a way' by Don Moen ©1990 Integrity's Hosanna! Music/Sovereign Music UK, PO Box 356, Leighton Buzzard, LU7 3WP, UK. Reproduced by permission.

74. John 10:27
75. Psalm 23
76. Pastor Albert Garner. Pastor Albert Garner has been the Senior Minister of The Gloucester Assemblies of God church since 1967.
77. John 14:15
78. Colossians 2:12
79. John 10:27
80. Genesis 2:18
81. Ephesians 4:28. Scripture taken from the HOLY BIBLE, NEW INTERNATIONAL VERSION. Copyright © 1973, 1978, 1984 by International Bible Society. Used by permission of Hodder & Stoughton, a member of Hodder Headline Ltd. All rights reserved.
82. Matthew 18:19
83. Jeremiah 33:3
84. Romans 8:31
85. Philippians 4:19. Scripture taken from KING JAMES VERSION. Copyright © 1970, 2001 by Thomas Nelson Inc. Used by permission.
86. 'Something Beautiful.' Words by Gloria Gaither. Music by William J. Gaither. Copyright © 1971 William J. Gaither Inc. © All rights controlled by Gaither Copyright Management. Used by permission.
87. Mark 1:15
88. Jeremiah 17:9. Scripture taken from KING JAMES VERSION. Copyright © 1970, 2001 by Thomas Nelson Inc. Used by permission.
89. Romans 3:23
90. 'Only by Grace' by Gerrit Gustafson Copyright © 1990 Integrity's Hosanna! Music/Sovereign Music UK, PO Box 356, Leighton Buzzard, LU7 3WP, UK. Reproduced by permission.
91. Romans 10:9

92. Matthew 13:44
93. Hebrews 13:5
94. Colossians 2:14
95. John 10:10
96. 'Jesus Makes the Difference in Me' source unknown.
97. 1 John 5:11–13
98. 2 Timothy 3:16–17
99. Philippians 4:6
100. Colossians 2:6
101. Ephesians 3:14–16
102. Matthew 10:32
103. Acts 2:44–46
104. Hebrews 10:25